MAXIMIZING HIGHER EDUCATION

The Solution to Economic and Financial Well-Being

The Reasons for Higher Education: Mastery and Income

DR LESTER G. REID

The Author of "Maximizing Put and Call Options Trading: The Secrets to Winning Each Put and Call Trading."

COPYRIGHT

The contents of this book, including but not limited to text, images, and illustrations, are protected under the copyright laws of United States of America and international conventions. The author and publisher have made every effort to ensure that the information provided in this book is accurate and up to date at the time of publication.

Unauthorized reproduction or distribution of any part of this book is prohibited. This includes but is not limited to copying, scanning, or distributing in any form or by any means, including electronic, mechanical, photocopying, recording, or otherwise, without the prior written permission of the author and publisher.

Dr. Lester Reid

ISBN: 978-1-7340601-7-1

Copyright © 2023

Global Higher Education Institute Publishing

ABOUT THIS BOOK

"Maximizing Higher Education: The Solution to Economic and Financial Well-Being" is a groundbreaking book that explores the crucial role of higher education in driving economic prosperity and financial well-being. This book examines the transformative power of education and offers insightful strategies to maximize its impact on individuals and society as a whole. By challenging conventional wisdom and providing evidence-based recommendations, this book serves as a thought-provoking resource for students, parents, educators, policymakers, and anyone interested in harnessing the potential of higher education for personal and societal advancement.

1. **Understanding the Importance of Higher Education:** The book begins by establishing the significance of higher education in an increasingly complex and interconnected world. It highlights how education has emerged as a cornerstone for personal growth, intellectual development, and professional success. By examining the transformative power of education, the book emphasizes the often-underestimated impact

of education on economic and financial well-being.

2. **Debunking Myths and Misconceptions:** "Maximizing Higher Education" confronts prevalent myths and misconceptions surrounding higher education. It provides a comprehensive analysis of the economic impact of education at both the individual and societal levels. By dispelling misconceptions, the book offers a more accurate understanding of the correlation between education, employment, entrepreneurship, and economic prosperity.

3. **Exploring the Interplay of Education and Economic Landscape:** The book examine the intricate interplay between education and the economic landscape. It sheds light on the key factors that contribute to the correlation between higher education and financial well-being. Through research, data-driven insights, and real-life examples, the book unravels the ways in which individuals and societies can harness the full potential of education to enhance their economic prospects.

4. **Navigating the Complex Landscape of Higher Education:** "Maximizing Higher Education" serves as a roadmap for readers to navigate the complex landscape of higher education. It offers guidance on making informed decisions regarding educational pursuits, such as choosing the right academic program, evaluating the return on investment, and leveraging educational opportunities for career advancement. The book empowers readers to approach higher education strategically, aligning their aspirations and circumstances with the available options.

5. **Addressing Inequalities and Barriers:** The book acknowledges the inherent inequalities and barriers that exist in accessing quality education and its subsequent economic benefits. It explores strategies to bridge these gaps, advocating for inclusive and equitable education systems. By emphasizing the importance of removing barriers to education, the book aims to contribute to the broader conversation on social mobility and economic empowerment.

6. **The Transformative Role of Education:** "Maximizing Higher Education" recognizes the transformative role that education can

play in breaking cycles of poverty and fostering sustainable development. It highlights how education can serve as a catalyst for personal and societal transformation, empowering individuals to unlock their full potential and contribute to economic growth and social progress.

7. **Diverse Perspectives and Evidence-Based Recommendations:** Throughout the book, readers encounter diverse perspectives, expert opinions, and evidence-based recommendations. This multifaceted approach provides a nuanced understanding of the intricate relationship between higher education and economic well-being. By presenting a range of viewpoints and supporting arguments with research and data, the book encourages critical thinking and informed decision-making.

8. **A Guidebook for Empowerment:** "Maximizing Higher Education" is not a one-size-fits-all solution but rather a guidebook for empowerment. It empowers readers to make informed decisions and take deliberate actions that align with their aspirations and circumstances. Whether readers are students, parents, educators, or policymakers, this

book equips them with the knowledge and insights needed to navigate the higher education landscape effectively.

"Maximizing Higher Education: The Solution to Economic and Financial Well-Being" is a timely and comprehensive exploration of the transformative power of higher education. Through its analysis of the interplay between education, employment, entrepreneurship, and economic prosperity, the book provides readers with the tools to maximize their educational experiences and unlock their full potential. By challenging prevailing narratives and offering evidence-based recommendations, this book paves the way for individuals and societies to leverage higher education as a catalyst for economic growth, social mobility, and personal fulfillment.

Table of Contents

CHAPTER ONE 13
Reasons for Higher Education: Mastery and Income 13
- To Become Masterful 19
- To Generate Income 20

What is Higher Education? 25
The Holistic Approach 29
Higher Education Curriculum 33
Pursuing Higher Education 38

CHAPTER TWO 48
Higher Education Institutions 48
Types of Higher Education Institutions 51
Choosing a Higher Education Institution 56
Gateway to Success – Higher Education 60
- *The Gap between Theory and Practice* 60
- *Implications of the Gap:* 62
- *Strategies to Bridge the Gap:* 63
- *The Importance of Practical Application* 66
- *Developing Transferable Skills* 72
- *Internships and Work Experience* 79
- *Networking and Mentoring* 94
- *Seeking Hands-On Learning Opportunities* 101
- *Embracing a Growth Mindset* 108
- *Emphasizing Experiential Learning* 116
- *Encouraging Critical Thinking and Problem-Solving* 116
- *Promoting Entrepreneurship and Innovation* 117
- *Collaborative and Interdisciplinary Learning* 117
- *Encouraging Reflective Practice* 118
- *Cultivating Professional Skills* 118
- *Engaging with Industry Partners* 118
- *Continuous Feedback and Assessment* 119

CHAPTER THREE 121
   Moving Away from Poverty 121
   Tired of Being Broke and In Need? 126
   Thirst for Economic and Financial Change 137
   The Myths about Higher Education 143

CHAPTER FOUR 150
   Famous Believers About Higher Education 150
   Things Employers SHOULD Do 161
   Things Employers Should NOT Do 172

100 Similar Words - Higher Education 177
   List of 500 Careers by Profession and Industry 181

Thought Provoking Quote 203

References 206

ABOUT THE AUTHOR 211

PREFACE

In today's complex and interconnected world, higher education has emerged as a crucial pillar for personal growth, intellectual development, and professional achievement. While the transformative nature of education has long been acknowledged, its profound impact on economic and financial well-being is often underestimated. It is this profound realization that has given birth to "Maximizing Higher Education: The Solution to Economic and Financial Well-Being."

This book sets out to explore the intricate relationship between higher education and the economic landscape, unraveling the myriad ways in which individuals and societies can harness the full potential of education to enhance their financial well-being. By examining the key factors that contribute to this correlation, it sheds light on the complex interplay between education, employment, entrepreneurship, and overall economic prosperity.

At its core, this book seeks to challenge the prevailing wisdom surrounding higher education and its connection to financial success. It confronts prevailing myths and misconceptions head-on, providing a comprehensive analysis of the economic impact of education at both the individual and societal levels. Through a synthesis of research, data-driven insights, and real-life examples, it equips readers with a roadmap to navigate the intricate landscape of higher education and make informed decisions regarding their educational pursuits.

"Maximizing Higher Education" also acknowledges the inherent inequalities and barriers that impede equitable access to quality education and its subsequent economic benefits. It explores strategies to bridge these gaps, advocating for inclusive and equitable education systems that empower individuals from all walks of life to unlock their full potential. By doing so, it aims to contribute to the broader discourse on social mobility and economic empowerment, emphasizing the transformative role that education can play in breaking the cycle of poverty and fostering sustainable development.

Throughout the pages of this book, readers will encounter diverse perspectives, expert opinions, and evidence-based recommendations. It is our sincere hope that this multifaceted approach will foster a nuanced understanding of the intricate relationship between higher education and economic well-being, transcending simplistic narratives and offering a more holistic view.

"Maximizing Higher Education: The Solution to Economic and Financial Well-Being" is not a one-size-fits-all solution or a panacea for all challenges. Rather, it serves as an empowering guidebook, enabling readers to make informed decisions and take intentional actions that align with their aspirations and circumstances. Whether you are a student, a parent, an educator, a policymaker, or simply someone intrigued by the transformative power of education, this book is intended to be a thought-provoking and illuminating resource.

I extend an invitation to embark on this journey of exploration, reflection, and discovery. Together, let us examine the realm of higher education and unlock its immense potential to shape a brighter and more prosperous future for individuals and societies alike.

CHAPTER ONE

Reasons for Higher Education: Mastery and Income

In contemporary society, the decision to pursue higher education is often driven by a multitude of factors, including personal aspirations, intellectual curiosity, and career prospects. While the acquisition of specialized knowledge and skills is undoubtedly one of the primary objectives, the expectation of earning a substantial income in the future is also a prevalent motivation. This book aims to examine the two central reasons behind attending college: to become masterful in one's field of study and to potentially earn a significant income throughout one's lifetime. By exploring these facets, we will gain a deeper understanding of the multifaceted nature and implications of pursuing higher education.

When considering the merits of pursuing higher education, two significant aspects often come to the forefront: mastery in one's chosen field and the potential for increased income. College offers a unique opportunity for individuals to examine deeply into their academic passions, expanding their knowledge and honing their skills to become masters in their respective disciplines. Simultaneously, it is widely recognized that a college education can open doors to lucrative career paths and higher earning potential. Together, we will explore these two facets of college, examining the pursuit of mastery and the potential for financial prosperity that often accompanies higher education.

Higher education, as a transformative journey, encompasses diverse dimensions that go beyond the acquisition of knowledge and skills. Among the myriad of motivations behind pursuing a college degree, two primary facets emerge: the pursuit of mastery in one's chosen field and the potential for increased income. These facets, intertwined and complementary, shape the narrative surrounding the value and impact of higher education.

College serves as a fertile ground for individuals to cultivate mastery in their chosen field of study. It provides a structured and immersive environment where students can examine the depths of knowledge, explore diverse perspectives, and engage in intellectual discourse. By immersing themselves in rigorous academic programs, students acquire a deep understanding of their discipline, develop critical thinking abilities, and refine their analytical skills. Through coursework, research projects, and practical experiences, they gain the expertise necessary to excel in their chosen field.

The pursuit of mastery extends beyond the accumulation of knowledge. It entails a commitment to continuous learning, growth, and the development of specialized skills. College acts as a catalyst for intellectual curiosity, nurturing an environment where students are encouraged to challenge existing paradigms, engage in critical inquiry, and push the boundaries of knowledge. By fostering a collaborative and interdisciplinary atmosphere, higher education institutions empower students to become lifelong learners, always seeking to deepen their understanding and refine their expertise.

Secondly, higher education offers the potential for increased income and enhanced career prospects. Attaining a college degree has long been associated with higher earning potential and improved employability. The specialized knowledge and skills acquired through higher education are highly valued by employers, positioning graduates as desirable candidates in the job market. Furthermore, certain fields, such as STEM (Science, Technology, Engineering, and Mathematics) disciplines and professional fields like medicine, law, and finance, often require advanced degrees for entry. These fields offer lucrative career paths where the acquisition of specialized knowledge translates into higher income opportunities.

Beyond the economic aspect, a college education equips individuals with transferable skills that are sought after in a wide range of industries. Skills such as critical thinking, problem-solving, communication, and teamwork are not only vital for professional success but also highly valued in today's dynamic and interconnected world. Higher education cultivates these skills, allowing graduates to adapt to evolving industries, navigate complex challenges, and seize opportunities for career advancement. However, it is crucial to recognize that the value of higher education extends beyond financial gain. College education fosters personal growth, broadens perspectives, and nurtures a sense of civic responsibility. It nurtures creativity, cultural appreciation, and social awareness, encouraging students to contribute meaningfully to society and make a positive impact in their communities.

One of the primary motivations for pursuing higher education is the desire to become masterful in a chosen field of study. College provides a unique environment where individuals can immerse themselves in their academic passions, gain in-depth knowledge, and develop expertise that sets them apart. The journey toward mastery is a transformative process that encompasses intellectual growth, skill development, and personal fulfillment. Primarily, higher education institutions offer a structured curriculum designed to cultivate mastery in various fields of study. Students engage in a comprehensive range of courses that provide a strong foundation in the theoretical frameworks and fundamental principles of their discipline. From the humanities to the sciences, each area of study offers a unique set of challenges and opportunities for exploration. Through coursework, students gain a deeper understanding of the subject matter, build a robust knowledge base, and develop critical thinking skills that are essential for mastery.

Beyond the classroom, colleges provide numerous opportunities for practical application and hands-on learning. Laboratory work, research projects, internships, and co-op programs offer students the chance to apply their theoretical knowledge in real-world contexts. These experiences foster a deeper understanding of the practical implications of their field, enhance problem-solving abilities, and develop crucial skills relevant to their future careers.

Another crucial aspect of becoming masterful in a field of study is the guidance and mentorship provided by experienced faculty members. Professors and mentors play a pivotal role in shaping students' intellectual development and helping them navigate their academic journey. Through one-on-one interactions, mentorship programs, and research collaborations, students can benefit from the wisdom, expertise, and insights of their mentors. This mentorship not only facilitates academic growth but also provides guidance for personal and professional development, offering invaluable support and inspiration along the path to mastery.

Moreover, the pursuit of mastery often extends beyond the confines of the classroom. Higher education institutions foster vibrant academic communities where students engage in intellectual discourse, collaborate on projects, and exchange ideas. Participating in academic clubs, attending seminars and conferences, and joining study groups provide avenues for intellectual stimulation and exposure to diverse perspectives. These interactions with peers and scholars create a rich and stimulating environment that fuels the pursuit of mastery and nurtures a lifelong passion for learning.

Furthermore, colleges often offer specialized programs, concentrations, and research opportunities that enable students to examine deeper into their chosen field. These programs allow individuals to explore specific areas of interest, conduct original research, and contribute to the advancement of knowledge in their discipline. By engaging in these focused pursuits, students gain specialized expertise, establish themselves as experts within narrower domains, and make meaningful contributions to the academic community.

To Become Masterful

Becoming masterful in a field of study is not only a personal goal but also has wider implications. Individuals who attain mastery often become leaders, innovators, and contributors to their respective fields. Their deep understanding and expertise enable them to tackle complex challenges, propose innovative solutions, and advance the boundaries of knowledge. By actively engaging with their discipline, they have the potential to make significant contributions to research, industry, and society at large.

Furthermore, the journey toward mastery fosters personal growth and fulfillment. It instills a sense of purpose, self-confidence, and resilience as individuals navigate the challenges and setbacks inherent in the pursuit of excellence. The process of becoming masterful involves perseverance, continuous learning, and a commitment to self-improvement. This personal development extends beyond the acquisition of knowledge and skills and encompasses qualities such as discipline, creativity, and adaptability that are essential for success in any endeavor.

The pursuit of mastery in a chosen field of study is a fundamental aspect of higher education. Colleges provide an environment conducive to intellectual growth, skill development, and personal fulfillment. Through a combination of structured coursework, practical experiences, mentorship, and engagement with academic communities, students can embark on a transformative journey toward becoming masterful. Beyond personal growth, attaining mastery carries wider significance, enabling individuals to make meaningful contributions to their field and society as a whole.

To Generate Income

One of the significant drivers behind the pursuit of higher education is the potential for increased income and the opportunity to secure lucrative career prospects. While financial gain should not be the sole measure of the value of education, it is an important consideration for many individuals. College graduates often enjoy higher earning potential compared to those with only a high school diploma, and higher education equips individuals with the knowledge, skills, and credentials necessary to access a broader range of career opportunities.

Primarily, a college education is associated with improved employability and higher chances of securing well-paying jobs. Employers often value the specialized knowledge and skills that come with a college degree, considering it a sign of dedication, commitment, and proficiency. The comprehensive education provided by higher education institutions prepares graduates for the demands of the modern workforce, equipping them with a broad set of transferable skills. These skills, such as critical thinking, problem-solving, communication, and teamwork, are highly sought after by employers across various industries.

Furthermore, certain professions require advanced degrees as a prerequisite for entry. Fields such as medicine, law, engineering, and finance often demand specialized knowledge and advanced training. Pursuing higher education in these disciplines not only enhances one's understanding but also opens doors to high-paying career paths. The acquisition of specialized degrees and certifications increases earning potential as individuals possess the expertise necessary to excel in these fields.

Moreover, the economic value of higher education is evident in the salary premiums that college graduates often enjoy. Numerous studies consistently show that individuals with a college degree earn higher incomes on average compared to those with only a high school diploma. The degree of income disparity between these groups can be substantial over a lifetime. A college education sets individuals on a trajectory toward higher-paying positions, providing opportunities for upward mobility and financial stability.

Furthermore, the potential for earning vast amounts of income is often influenced by the choice of major or area of specialization. Some fields, such as STEM (Science, Technology, Engineering, and Mathematics) disciplines, computer science, and business, are known to offer high-paying careers. Graduates in these fields typically command competitive salaries due to the demand for their skills and expertise.

However, it is important to note that earning potential is not solely dependent on the choice of major. Factors such as individual capabilities, industry trends, geographic location, and market conditions also influence income levels. Beyond the immediate financial benefits, a higher income can have long-term effects on an individual's financial well-being and quality of life. Higher earning potential allows individuals to accumulate wealth, invest in their future, and enjoy a higher standard of living. It provides opportunities for economic security, homeownership, and access to better healthcare and educational opportunities for themselves and their families.

However, it is crucial to approach the relationship between higher education and income with a nuanced perspective. While a college education can enhance earning potential, it is not a guarantee of financial success. Economic outcomes can be influenced by various factors, including market conditions, personal circumstances, and individual effort. The value of education extends beyond monetary gain, encompassing personal growth, social mobility, and the acquisition of knowledge that contributes to a well-rounded and fulfilling life.

Moreover, the pursuit of higher education should not solely be driven by financial motives. It is essential to consider one's passions, interests, and personal goals when choosing a field of study. A fulfilling and meaningful career is often built on a foundation of genuine enthusiasm for the work and a sense of purpose. While financial considerations play a role, aligning one's educational pursuits with personal interests and values can lead to long-term satisfaction and a sense of fulfillment in one's chosen profession.

The potential for earning vast amounts of income is a compelling aspect of higher education. College graduates often enjoy improved employability, higher earning potential, and access to a broader range of career opportunities. Higher education equips individuals with the knowledge, skills, and credentials necessary to succeed in today's competitive job market. However, it is important to approach the pursuit of higher education holistically, considering personal passions, individual circumstances, and long-term goals. While financial considerations are significant, the value of education extends beyond income, encompassing personal growth, social mobility, and the pursuit of a fulfilling and meaningful career.

The two facets of mastery and income form the foundations of the multifaceted value of higher education. College serves as a transformative journey where individuals strive to become masters in their chosen fields while simultaneously positioning themselves for increased income and career opportunities. It is important to acknowledge that the benefits of higher education extend beyond financial gain, encompassing personal growth, societal contributions, and the holistic development of individuals. As we explore the complexities and nuances of the role of higher education in society, understanding and appreciating the interconnectedness of these facets will lead to a more comprehensive view of the transformative power of a college education.

What is Higher Education?

Higher education is an educational pursuit beyond the secondary level, typically referring to educational programs and institutions that offer undergraduate and postgraduate degrees. It encompasses a wide range of academic disciplines, vocational training, and professional development opportunities. Higher education institutions, such as universities, colleges, and technical schools, provide a platform for individuals to deepen their knowledge, acquire specialized skills, and engage in intellectual exploration.

At its core, higher education is a transformative journey that goes beyond the acquisition of knowledge. It fosters personal growth, intellectual development, and the cultivation of critical thinking skills. Through rigorous coursework, research projects, practical experiences, and engagement with academic communities, students are encouraged to question, analyze, and challenge prevailing ideas. Higher education provides an environment where students can engage in intellectual discourse, broaden their perspectives, and develop a deeper understanding of the world around them.

Higher education offers a diverse range of programs and degrees tailored to individual interests and career aspirations. Undergraduate programs, such as Bachelor's degrees, provide a broad foundation in various fields of study. They often include general education requirements to ensure a well-rounded education and allow students to explore different disciplines before focusing on a specific major. Graduate programs, including Master's and doctoral degrees, offer advanced study in specialized fields, allowing individuals to deepen their expertise and engage in advanced research.

The value of higher education extends beyond academic knowledge and encompasses the development of transferable skills. Skills such as critical thinking, problem-solving, communication, teamwork, and adaptability are highly valued in today's rapidly changing workforce. Higher education equips individuals with these skills, enhancing their employability and preparing them for the challenges of the modern job market.

Furthermore, higher education institutions foster a vibrant community of scholars, educators, and students. They serve as hubs of intellectual activity, facilitating the exchange of ideas, interdisciplinary collaborations, and the pursuit of innovative research. Students have the opportunity to engage with faculty members, experts in their respective fields, who provide guidance, mentorship, and support in their academic journey. The academic community within higher education institutions nurtures a spirit of inquiry, intellectual curiosity, and lifelong learning.

Higher education also plays a significant role in promoting social mobility and addressing societal challenges. It offers opportunities for individuals from diverse backgrounds to access quality education and break barriers that may otherwise limit their potential. By providing an inclusive and equitable learning environment, higher education institutions contribute to the development of a more diverse and inclusive society. Furthermore, higher education institutions often engage in research and community outreach initiatives, addressing pressing social issues, and contributing to the betterment of society.

It is important to note that higher education is not limited to traditional classroom-based learning. Technological advancements have expanded educational opportunities, giving rise to online learning platforms, distance education programs, and hybrid learning models. These alternative approaches to higher education offer flexibility and accessibility, allowing individuals to pursue educational opportunities regardless of geographical location or time constraints.

Higher education is a transformative and multifaceted journey that provides individuals with the opportunity to acquire knowledge, develop skills, and engage in intellectual exploration. It encompasses undergraduate and graduate programs, vocational training, and professional development opportunities. Higher education institutions serve as catalysts for personal growth, intellectual development, and the cultivation of critical thinking skills. Beyond academic knowledge, higher education equips individuals with transferable skills and enhances their employability. Moreover, it promotes social mobility, fosters an inclusive learning environment, and addresses societal challenges. As the landscape of education continues to evolve, higher education remains a vital force in shaping individuals, communities, and societies as a whole.

The Holistic Approach

The holistic approach to higher education encompasses a broader perspective that goes beyond the acquisition of knowledge and skills. It recognizes the significance of human development and advancement, emphasizing the holistic growth of individuals as they navigate their educational journey. This approach encompasses various dimensions of personal, intellectual, and emotional development, fostering a well-rounded and empowered individual.

Higher education institutions play a crucial role in facilitating holistic development by providing a supportive environment for students to thrive intellectually, emotionally, and socially. Through a combination of academic programs, extracurricular activities, and support services, they aim to cultivate the overall well-being and personal growth of students.

One key aspect of the holistic approach to higher education is the emphasis on personal growth and self-discovery. Colleges and universities often offer opportunities for students to explore their passions, values, and interests outside of their academic pursuits. Extracurricular activities, clubs, and student organizations provide avenues for students to develop leadership skills, build meaningful relationships, and engage in activities that align with their personal interests. These experiences foster self-awareness, encourage self-expression, and contribute to the overall personal development of students.

Furthermore, the holistic approach recognizes the importance of emotional and social development in higher education. College can be a transformative period in an individual's life, often characterized by newfound independence and personal growth. Higher education institutions provide resources and support services, such as counseling centers and student wellness programs, to help students navigate the challenges of academic life and promote their emotional well-being. By addressing the mental health needs of students, colleges aim to create an environment that nurtures resilience, emotional intelligence, and interpersonal skills.

Intellectual development is also central to the holistic approach to higher education. While the acquisition of knowledge and specialized skills is an important aspect, the focus extends beyond rote learning and memorization. Higher education institutions strive to foster critical thinking, problem-solving, and analytical skills that enable students to think independently, question assumptions, and engage in intellectual inquiry. The curriculum is designed to encourage interdisciplinary learning, promote creativity, and cultivate a deeper understanding of complex issues. Through research projects, collaborative learning experiences, and exposure to diverse perspectives, students develop the intellectual agility and adaptability necessary for success in the modern world.

Moreover, to personal and intellectual development, the holistic approach recognizes the importance of ethical and moral development. Higher education institutions aim to instill values such as integrity, social responsibility, and ethical decision-making in their students. They provide opportunities for students to engage in community service, internships, and experiential learning that promote a sense of civic engagement and social justice. By encouraging students to apply their knowledge and skills to real-world issues, colleges foster a commitment to making a positive impact on society.

The holistic approach to higher education also acknowledges the significance of lifelong learning and continuous personal development. In an ever-evolving world, individuals need to adapt, learn new skills, and stay abreast of emerging trends and technologies. Higher education institutions promote a culture of lifelong learning by offering professional development programs, continuing education courses, and opportunities for alumni engagement. This commitment to lifelong learning enables individuals to remain competitive in the job market and navigate the complexities of the ever-changing professional landscape.

Moreover, the holistic approach recognizes the interconnectedness between individuals, communities, and the environment. Higher education institutions increasingly emphasize sustainability, global awareness, and cultural competency. They strive to provide students with the knowledge and understanding of global issues, cross-cultural perspectives, and the importance of environmental stewardship. By fostering a global mindset and promoting social responsibility, colleges contribute to the development of well-rounded individuals who are equipped to address complex global challenges.

The holistic approach to higher education goes beyond the traditional notions of knowledge acquisition and skill development. It emphasizes the holistic growth and development of individuals, encompassing personal, intellectual, emotional, and ethical dimensions. Higher education institutions play a vital role in creating an environment that fosters personal growth, promotes emotional well-being, and cultivates critical thinking skills. By embracing a holistic approach, colleges and universities empower individuals to become well-rounded, socially responsible, and lifelong learners. This approach not only prepares individuals for successful careers but also contributes to their personal fulfillment and the betterment of society as a whole.

Higher Education Curriculum

The curriculum in higher education plays a significant role in shaping students' personal development, fostering growth, and preparing them for future endeavors. While the acquisition of knowledge and specialized skills is essential, a well-designed curriculum goes beyond the transfer of information and focuses on holistic personal development. It incorporates various elements that nurture critical thinking, creativity, self-awareness, interpersonal skills, and a sense of social responsibility.

Higher education curriculum encourages critical thinking and analytical skills, empowering students to question assumptions, evaluate evidence, and engage in independent thought. Courses are designed to challenge students intellectually, exposing them to diverse perspectives and encouraging them to analyze complex issues from multiple angles. Through class discussions, research projects, and assignments that require critical analysis, students develop the ability to think critically, form reasoned arguments, and make informed decisions. This fosters intellectual growth and equips students with the skills necessary for problem-solving and decision-making in their future personal and professional lives.

Creativity is another important aspect of personal development that a higher education curriculum can nurture. Many disciplines within higher education require students to think creatively, innovate, and approach problems from fresh perspectives. Courses in the arts, humanities, and sciences often encourage creativity by promoting original thought, experimentation, and the exploration of alternative solutions. Engaging in creative endeavors fosters self-expression, imagination, and the ability to see beyond conventional boundaries. By integrating opportunities for creative expression within the curriculum, higher education institutions empower students to develop their unique voices and contribute to their chosen fields.

Moreover, a well-designed curriculum in higher education emphasizes self-awareness and personal growth. Courses and programs often include components that encourage reflection, introspection, and self-assessment. Students may be prompted to reflect on their values, strengths, and areas for improvement. These exercises foster self-awareness and help students understand their own motivations, aspirations, and personal development goals. By integrating self-reflection into the curriculum, higher education institutions enable students to develop a deeper understanding of themselves, make more informed choices, and pursue meaningful paths aligned with their values and passions.

Interpersonal skills and social intelligence are also vital aspects of personal development addressed by higher education curricula. Collaborative projects, group discussions, and experiential learning opportunities provide students with opportunities to develop effective communication, teamwork, and leadership skills. Through these experiences, students learn to navigate diverse perspectives, work effectively with others, and develop empathy and cultural sensitivity. These interpersonal skills are crucial for success in personal relationships, teamwork, and professional settings, and they contribute to students' personal growth and overall well-being.

Furthermore, a higher education curriculum can incorporate components that foster a sense of social responsibility and a commitment to making a positive impact on society. Courses that explore societal issues, ethics, sustainability, and social justice encourage students to think beyond their personal interests and consider the broader implications of their actions. Experiential learning opportunities, such as community service projects, internships, and service-learning courses, provide students with firsthand experiences of working towards social change. These experiences cultivate a sense of social responsibility, civic engagement, and an understanding of the role individuals can play in addressing societal challenges.

Furthermore, higher education curricula can include elements that promote personal well-being and mental health. Recognizing the importance of emotional well-being in personal development, colleges and universities may incorporate courses or programs that address stress management, emotional intelligence, mindfulness, and self-care. By providing resources and opportunities for students to develop strategies for self-care and stress reduction, institutions contribute to the overall well-being and personal growth of students.

Higher education curricula have the potential to shape students' personal development by going beyond the acquisition of knowledge and specialized skills. A well-designed curriculum integrates elements that foster critical thinking, creativity, self-awareness, interpersonal skills, and a sense of social responsibility. By providing opportunities for reflection, collaboration, experiential learning, and exposure to diverse perspectives, higher education institutions contribute to students' intellectual growth, personal fulfillment, and overall well-being. A holistic approach to curriculum design ensures that students leave higher education with not only academic expertise but also the personal and interpersonal skills necessary for success in their future endeavors and the ability to make positive contributions to society.

Pursuing Higher Education

While pursuing higher education at higher education institutions, there are numerous opportunities and activities that can enhance your overall experience and contribute to personal and professional growth. Here are some suggestions on what to do during your higher education journey:

1. **Engage in Academic Excellence:** Make the most of your educational experience by actively participating in your courses, attending lectures, and actively engaging in discussions. Strive for academic excellence by studying diligently, completing assignments on time, and seeking clarification when needed. Take advantage of resources such as libraries, research facilities, and online databases to deepen your knowledge and understanding of your field of study.

2. **Join Student Organizations and Clubs:** Participating in student organizations and clubs allows you to connect with like-minded individuals, develop leadership skills, and engage in extracurricular activities. Join clubs related to your interests, academic discipline, or hobbies. These groups offer

opportunities to collaborate on projects, organize events, and develop teamwork and organizational skills.

3. **Seek Internship and Work Experience:** Internships and work experience provide valuable opportunities to apply classroom knowledge in real-world settings. Look for internships, co-op programs, or part-time jobs relevant to your field of study. These experiences not only enhance your skills but also allow you to network with professionals, gain practical insights, and build a strong foundation for future employment.

4. **Participate in Research Projects:** If you have a passion for research, seek opportunities to collaborate with professors or join research projects within your department. Engaging in research enhances critical thinking, problem-solving, and analytical skills. It also allows you to examine deeper into your area of interest and contribute to the advancement of knowledge in your field.

5. **Take Advantage of Study Abroad Programs:** Many higher education institutions offer study abroad programs that

allow you to explore different cultures, gain a global perspective, and develop intercultural competence. Studying abroad provides opportunities for personal growth, cross-cultural understanding, and expanding your professional network. It broadens your horizons and enhances your adaptability and resilience.

6. **Build Relationships with Faculty and Mentors:** Developing strong relationships with faculty members and mentors can greatly benefit your academic and professional journey. Seek guidance from professors, engage in discussions outside of the classroom, and participate in research projects or mentorship programs. Faculty members can offer valuable insights, career advice, and letters of recommendation that can support your future endeavors.

7. **Network with Peers and Professionals:** Networking is crucial for personal and professional growth. Attend career fairs, industry events, and alumni gatherings to connect with professionals in your field. Join professional associations and engage in online communities related to your industry. Networking allows you to learn from

experienced professionals, explore career opportunities, and build a strong professional network that can open doors to future collaborations and job prospects.

8. **Develop Transferable Skills:** Moreover, to your academic studies, focus on developing transferable skills that are valued by employers across various industries. These skills include communication, teamwork, problem-solving, critical thinking, and leadership. Look for opportunities to enhance these skills through workshops, seminars, volunteering, or leadership roles in student organizations.

9. **Prioritize Self-Care and Wellness:** While pursuing higher education, it's important to prioritize self-care and wellness. Take breaks, engage in physical activities, and maintain a healthy work-life balance. Seek support from counseling services or student support centers if needed. Prioritizing your well-being ensures that you can perform at your best academically and maintain overall personal happiness.

10. **Embrace Diversity and Cultural Exchange:** Higher education institutions are

diverse and inclusive communities. Embrace the opportunity to learn from individuals with different backgrounds, cultures, and perspectives. Engage in conversations that promote understanding, empathy, and respect. Participate in events and initiatives that celebrate diversity and promote inclusivity on campus.

Pursuing higher education at higher education institutions is a transformative journey that extends beyond the classroom. By actively engaging in academic excellence, participating in student organizations, seeking internships and research opportunities, building relationships, networking, developing transferable skills, and prioritizing wellness, you can make the most of your higher education experience. Embrace the opportunities available, expand your horizons, and pave the way for a successful and fulfilling future.

Overcome Challenges

The pursuit of higher education is a transformative journey filled with opportunities for personal and professional growth. However, it is not without its challenges and disruptions. From academic difficulties to personal setbacks, navigating the higher education landscape requires resilience, adaptability, and a proactive approach. Together, we will explore strategies and practical steps to overcome challenges and disruptions while pursuing higher education, ensuring a successful and fulfilling academic journey.

1. **Embrace a Growth Mindset:** One of the most effective ways to overcome challenges is by cultivating a growth mindset. Embrace the belief that challenges are opportunities for growth and learning rather than insurmountable obstacles. Adopting a positive attitude towards setbacks will help you approach challenges with resilience and perseverance, allowing you to adapt and find creative solutions.

2. **Seek Support and Build a Supportive Network:** It is crucial to seek support when facing challenges in higher education. Reach out to professors, academic advisors, or student support services on campus for guidance and assistance. They can provide valuable advice, resources, and support to help you overcome academic or personal obstacles. Furthermore, build a network of peers who can offer encouragement, share experiences, and provide a sense of camaraderie throughout your journey.

3. **Develop Effective Time Management Skills:** Effective time management is essential for overcoming disruptions and maintaining academic success. Create a schedule that includes dedicated time for studying, attending classes, completing assignments, and engaging in extracurricular activities. Prioritize tasks, set realistic goals, and break them down into manageable steps. By managing your time effectively, you can reduce stress, stay organized, and make progress even in the face of challenges.

4. **Adapt to Remote Learning and Online Platforms:** In recent times, remote learning and online platforms have become increasingly prevalent. To overcome disruptions caused by such transitions, adapt to the digital learning environment. Familiarize yourself with online tools, establish a conducive study environment, and develop effective online communication and collaboration skills. Embrace the flexibility and opportunities that online learning provides while staying motivated and engaged in your studies.

5. **Develop Resilience and Perseverance:** Challenges and disruptions are inevitable in any educational journey. Building resilience and perseverance is key to overcoming these obstacles. Remind yourself of your goals, stay focused on your purpose, and maintain a positive mindset even when faced with setbacks. Use setbacks as opportunities for self-reflection, growth, and improvement. Remember that setbacks do not define your journey; it is your ability to bounce back and persevere that will lead to success.

6. **Seek Alternative Learning Resources:** When faced with challenges in understanding course material or specific subjects, seek alternative learning resources. Utilize online tutorials, educational websites, and video lectures to supplement your learning. Seek out study groups or tutoring services on campus. Exploring alternative resources can provide different perspectives and approaches to the material, enhancing your understanding and helping you overcome academic challenges.

7. **Practice Self-Care and Stress Management:** Taking care of your physical, mental, and emotional well-being is crucial in

overcoming challenges. Make self-care a priority by maintaining a balanced lifestyle. Engage in regular physical exercise, practice mindfulness or meditation, and engage in activities that bring you joy and relaxation. Prioritize sleep, eat nutritious meals, and seek support from friends, family, or counselors when needed. By managing stress and caring for yourself, you can approach challenges with a clear mind and renewed energy.

8. **Set Realistic Expectations and Celebrate Milestones:** Setting realistic expectations is vital to maintaining motivation and overcoming challenges. Break down your long-term goals into smaller, achievable milestones. Celebrate each milestone, no matter how small, as it signifies progress and growth. Recognize your achievements along the way, boosting your confidence and providing a sense of accomplishment that can propel you forward during challenging times.

Overcoming challenges and disruptions while pursuing higher education requires determination, resilience, and a proactive mindset. By embracing a growth mindset, seeking support, developing time management skills, adapting to new learning environments, building resilience, seeking alternative resources, practicing self-care, and setting realistic expectations, you can navigate your higher education journey successfully. Remember that challenges are opportunities for growth and that with perseverance and a positive mindset, you can overcome any obstacle that comes your way. Embrace the transformative power of higher education, and let your challenges be stepping stones to a brighter and more fulfilling academic journey.

CHAPTER TWO

Higher Education Institutions

Higher education institutions play a crucial role in providing individuals with the opportunity to pursue advanced education and acquire the knowledge and skills necessary for personal and professional success. These institutions encompass a diverse range of options, including trade schools, technical colleges, and four-year colleges. Each type of institution offers unique educational pathways tailored to different career goals and interests.

Trade schools, also known as vocational schools or career colleges, specialize in providing practical, hands-on training in specific trades or occupations. These institutions focus on equipping students with the skills required for immediate entry into the workforce. Trade schools typically offer programs in areas such as automotive technology, culinary arts, cosmetology, plumbing, electrical work, and construction. The curriculum emphasizes practical training and applied learning, preparing students to excel in their chosen fields. Trade schools are well-suited for individuals seeking to gain specialized skills in a relatively short period and enter the workforce quickly.

Technical colleges, also referred to as community colleges or two-year colleges, offer a wide range of educational programs, including associate degrees, certificates, and diplomas. Technical colleges provide a more comprehensive education compared to trade schools, combining technical training with general education courses. These institutions offer programs in fields such as healthcare, business, information technology, engineering technology, and many others. Technical colleges often have close ties with local industries and employers, ensuring that their curriculum aligns with workforce needs. Many students choose technical colleges as a cost-effective option to complete the first two years of their bachelor's degree before transferring to a four-year college or university.

Four-year colleges and universities are perhaps the most well-known higher education institutions. They offer a broad range of undergraduate and graduate programs across various disciplines, including liberal arts, sciences, business, engineering, humanities, and more. Four-year colleges typically confer bachelor's degrees upon completion of a four-year program of study. Universities, on the other hand, often consist of multiple colleges and schools, offering a wider array of programs, including bachelor's, master's, and doctoral degrees. These institutions emphasize a well-rounded education, combining general education requirements with specialized coursework in students' chosen fields of study. Four-year colleges and universities provide a comprehensive academic experience, emphasizing critical thinking, research, and in-depth analysis. They also offer a variety of extracurricular activities, research opportunities, and a vibrant campus life.

Moreover, to trade schools, technical colleges, and four-year colleges, there are other types of higher education institutions that cater to specific educational needs and career aspirations. These include professional schools, graduate schools, online universities, and specialized institutions such as art schools, music conservatories, and design schools. Professional schools, such as law schools, medical schools, and business schools, offer advanced degrees and specialized training in specific professions. Graduate schools provide opportunities for individuals to pursue master's and doctoral degrees, focusing on advanced research and scholarship. Online universities offer flexibility in terms of learning, allowing students to complete their education remotely through online platforms.

Specialized institutions focus on specific fields of study and provide in-depth training and education tailored to those disciplines.

Types of Higher Education Institutions

Higher education institutions play a crucial role in providing individuals with the opportunity to pursue advanced education and acquire the knowledge and skills necessary for personal and professional success. These institutions encompass a diverse range of options, including universities, colleges, and specialized schools. Each type of institution offers unique educational pathways tailored to different career goals and interests. Here are several examples of higher education institutions:

1. **Harvard University:** Harvard University, located in Cambridge, Massachusetts, is one of the world's most renowned institutions. It is a private Ivy League research university offering a wide range of undergraduate and graduate programs across various disciplines. Harvard is known for its excellence in fields such as law, business, medicine, public policy, and the humanities. The university boasts prestigious schools and faculties, including Harvard Business School, Harvard

Law School, Harvard Medical School, and Harvard College.

2. **Stanford University:** Situated in Stanford, California, Stanford University is a leading research institution recognized for its academic excellence and innovation. The university offers a diverse range of undergraduate and graduate programs in fields such as engineering, computer science, social sciences, humanities, and medicine. Stanford's prominent schools include the School of Engineering, School of Humanities and Sciences, and Graduate School of Business.

3. **Massachusetts Institute of Technology (MIT):** MIT, located in Cambridge, Massachusetts, is renowned for its focus on science, technology, engineering, and mathematics (STEM) education. The university offers undergraduate and graduate programs in fields such as engineering, computer science, biology, economics, and architecture. MIT is recognized for its cutting-edge research, technological advancements, and interdisciplinary approach to education.

4. **University of Oxford:** The University of Oxford, located in Oxford, England, is one of the oldest and most prestigious universities in the world. It is known for its rigorous academic programs and commitment to intellectual exploration. Oxford offers a wide range of undergraduate and graduate programs across various disciplines, including humanities, social sciences, natural sciences, and medical sciences. The university is comprised of several colleges, each with its own unique identity and traditions.

5. **University of California, Berkeley:** The University of California, Berkeley, is a renowned public research university located in Berkeley, California. It is part of the University of California system and offers a comprehensive range of undergraduate and graduate programs. Berkeley is recognized for its strength in fields such as engineering, computer science, social sciences, business, and the arts. The university is renowned for its vibrant campus life, commitment to social activism, and world-class faculty.

6. **Juilliard School:** The Juilliard School, situated in New York City, is a prestigious institution dedicated to the performing arts. It is renowned for its programs in music, dance, and drama. Juilliard provides intensive conservatory-style training to aspiring artists, preparing them for successful careers in the performing arts industry. The school's alumni include numerous celebrated musicians, actors, and dancers.

7. **Pratt Institute:** Pratt Institute, located in Brooklyn, New York, is a leading art and design college. It offers undergraduate and graduate programs in fields such as architecture, fine arts, design, and liberal arts. Pratt Institute is known for its focus on creativity, innovation, and hands-on learning. It prepares students for careers in various creative industries, including architecture, fashion design, graphic design, and industrial design.

8. **Community College of Denver:** The Community College of Denver (CCD) is a public community college in Denver, Colorado. It offers a wide range of associate degree and certificate programs in areas such as business, healthcare, criminal justice,

computer science, and liberal arts. CCD provides accessible and affordable education to students, serving as a gateway to higher education and workforce development.

9. **Southern New Hampshire University:** Southern New Hampshire University (SNHU) is a private, nonprofit university based in Manchester, New Hampshire. SNHU offers a variety of undergraduate and graduate programs, including online and on-campus options. The university is known for its flexible learning models and emphasis on career-focused education. SNHU provides diverse programs in fields such as business, education, healthcare, and technology.

10. **Fashion Institute of Technology (FIT):** The Fashion Institute of Technology, located in New York City, is a renowned institution for art, business, design, and technology in the fashion industry. It offers programs in areas such as fashion design, fashion merchandising, advertising and marketing communications, and visual arts. FIT provides hands-on training, industry partnerships, and opportunities for students to showcase their work during prestigious fashion events.

These examples represent the diversity of higher education institutions, each offering unique educational experiences and specialized areas of focus. It is important to note that there are numerous other notable institutions around the world, each with its own strengths, specializations, and academic offerings. The choice of a higher education institution depends on an individual's interests, career aspirations, location preferences, and educational goals.

Choosing a Higher Education Institution

Determining the "best" higher education institution for the desire to earn a relentless amount of income is a complex and subjective matter. Various factors come into play when considering the relationship between education and income, including the chosen field of study, individual capabilities and motivation, market demand, and personal circumstances. While certain institutions may have a reputation for producing high-earning graduates, it is essential to approach this topic with a nuanced perspective.

Primarily, it is important to recognize that the potential for high income is not solely determined by the institution attended but is influenced by multiple factors. The choice of field of study and specialization plays a significant role in income potential. Some fields, such as medicine, law, engineering, and finance, are known to offer high-paying careers. However, it is important to consider personal aptitude, passion, and alignment with career goals when choosing a field of study. Pursuing a career solely for its earning potential may lead to dissatisfaction and burnout in the long run.

While prestigious institutions often have strong networks, resources, and opportunities that can enhance career prospects, it is essential to note that success is not guaranteed by attending a particular institution. The skills, knowledge, and experiences gained during one's educational journey, along with personal motivation and dedication, play a vital role in career advancement and income growth.

Furthermore, the value of an education extends beyond immediate income potential. Higher education provides a comprehensive learning experience, fostering personal growth, critical thinking skills, and intellectual development. It equips individuals with a broad set of transferable skills, such as problem-solving, communication, and teamwork, which are highly valued by employers. A well-rounded education can open doors to a range of career opportunities and provide a solid foundation for long-term success.

That being said, some higher education institutions are known for their strong programs in fields that typically offer high income potential. For example, top-tier business schools, such as Harvard Business School and Stanford Graduate School of Business, have a reputation for producing graduates who achieve significant financial success. Similarly, prestigious engineering schools like the Massachusetts Institute of Technology (MIT) and California Institute of Technology (Caltech) often lead to lucrative careers in the engineering and technology sectors.

Moreover, to these examples, universities with strong programs in computer science, economics, finance, and other STEM fields often attract high-paying job opportunities. Institutions like Carnegie Mellon University, the University of California, Berkeley, and the University of Oxford are recognized for their excellence in these areas and have produced successful graduates who have achieved significant financial success.

It is important to note that the income potential associated with higher education is also influenced by regional and industry-specific factors. Different regions and countries may offer varying income levels based on their economic conditions and cost of living. Industries such as technology, finance, consulting, and healthcare tend to offer higher salaries compared to others. Thus, considering the location and industry trends is crucial when assessing income potential.

Moreover, the concept of earning a relentless amount of income should be balanced with other important factors, such as job satisfaction, work-life balance, and personal fulfillment. While financial success is undoubtedly important, it should not overshadow other aspects of a fulfilling career. Finding a career that aligns with personal interests, values, and passions often leads to long-term satisfaction and success.

Determining the "best" higher education institution for the desire to earn a relentless amount of income requires careful consideration of multiple factors. While certain institutions may have a reputation for producing high-earning graduates, income potential is influenced by individual capabilities, the chosen field of study, market demand, and personal circumstances. Pursuing education solely for its earning potential may overlook other important aspects of personal and professional fulfillment. Ultimately, the key to long-term success lies in finding a balance between financial aspirations, personal interests, and career satisfaction.

Gateway to Success – Higher Education

Obtaining a college degree is often seen as a gateway to success, promising better job prospects, higher earning potential, and a fulfilling career. However, many individuals find themselves disillusioned when their college degree fails to deliver the expected outcomes. One significant factor contributing to this disconnect is the lack of knowledge on how and when to apply the knowledge acquired during their educational journey. Together, we will explore why this discrepancy occurs and examine strategies for effectively applying the knowledge gained from a college degree to achieve professional success.

The Gap between Theory and Practice

One of the fundamental challenges faced by college graduates is the gap between theoretical knowledge acquired in classrooms and the practical application of that knowledge in real-world scenarios. Traditional higher education systems often prioritize theoretical concepts and academic performance, leaving little room for hands-on experiences and practical skill development. As a result, graduates may struggle to translate their theoretical understanding into practical applications when entering the workforce.

The gap between theory and practice is a well-known challenge in education and professional settings. While theoretical knowledge provides a foundation of understanding, practical application is essential for truly mastering a subject and successfully navigating real-world challenges. Together, we will explore the gap between theory and practice, its implications, and strategies to bridge this divide, fostering meaningful learning experiences and enhancing the application of knowledge.

The gap between theory and practice arises due to the inherent differences between academic learning and real-world situations. Theoretical knowledge is often obtained through lectures, textbooks, and structured educational environments. While this foundation is crucial, it can be limited in preparing individuals for the complexities, uncertainties, and unique circumstances encountered in practical settings.

Implications of the Gap:

1. Limited Application: Theoretical knowledge, when not applied practically, remains abstract and disconnected from its intended purpose. This limits its relevance and effectiveness in solving real-world problems.

2. Ineffective Decision-Making: In the absence of practical application, individuals may struggle to make informed decisions or develop effective strategies, as they lack experience in navigating complex situations.

3. Lack of Adaptability: Theoretical knowledge alone may not equip individuals with the skills to adapt to unexpected challenges, change course when necessary, or respond to dynamic circumstances.

4. Skill Gaps: Theoretical learning may not adequately address the development of skills required for specific tasks or professions, such as problem-solving, critical thinking, and effective communication.

5. Reduced Engagement: When theory is not effectively connected to practical application, individuals may become disengaged,

perceiving their learning as irrelevant or disconnected from the real world.

Strategies to Bridge the Gap:

1. **Experiential Learning:** Incorporate experiential learning methods such as internships, simulations, case studies, and hands-on projects that enable learners to apply theoretical concepts in practical settings. This helps bridge the gap by providing a context for knowledge application and fostering critical thinking and problem-solving skills.

2. **Real-World Examples:** Use real-world examples and case studies during teaching to illustrate the application of theoretical concepts. By presenting concrete situations, learners can better grasp how theory translates into practice.

3. **Collaborative Projects:** Encourage collaborative projects and group work that simulate real-world scenarios. This allows learners to engage in teamwork, communication, and collective problem-

solving, promoting the integration of theory and practice.

4. **Industry Partnerships:** Forge partnerships with industry organizations, professionals, and practitioners. These collaborations can provide opportunities for learners to gain firsthand experience, receive mentorship, and understand the practical applications of their knowledge.

5. **Reflection and Debates:** Incorporate reflection activities and debates that encourage learners to critically analyze the application of theory. This promotes metacognition and helps bridge the gap by enabling learners to connect their knowledge to practical contexts.

6. **Professional Practitioners as Educators:** Invite professionals from relevant fields to share their experiences and insights with learners. This enriches the learning experience by providing real-world perspectives, practical tips, and industry-specific knowledge.

7. **Internships and Apprenticeships:** Facilitate internships and apprenticeship

programs that allow learners to work in real-world environments under the guidance of experienced professionals. These experiences offer practical application, skill development, and networking opportunities.

8. **Mentorship Programs:** Establish mentorship programs connecting learners with experienced professionals who can provide guidance and support in navigating the practical aspects of their chosen field. This helps bridge the gap by facilitating the transfer of knowledge and industry-specific insights.

9. **Capstone Projects:** Implement capstone projects or culminating experiences that require learners to integrate and apply their theoretical knowledge to solve real-world problems. These projects promote deep learning and the practical application of acquired knowledge.

10. **Continuous Feedback and Assessment:** Provide regular feedback and assessment that focuses not only on theoretical understanding but also on the practical application of knowledge. This helps learners identify areas

for improvement and strengthen their ability to apply theory in practice.

Bridging the gap between theory and practice is crucial for meaningful learning experiences and the effective application of knowledge. By incorporating experiential learning, real-world examples, collaborative projects, industry partnerships, reflection activities, and mentorship programs, educators and institutions can help learners develop the skills, competencies, and confidence required to bridge this gap successfully. By nurturing a learning environment that emphasizes the application of knowledge, individuals will be better equipped to address complex challenges, make informed decisions, and thrive in real-world contexts.

The Importance of Practical Application

To succeed in today's dynamic and competitive job market, it is essential to bridge the gap between theory and practice. Merely possessing knowledge without the ability to apply it effectively diminishes the value of a college degree. Employers are increasingly seeking candidates who can not only demonstrate theoretical knowledge but also exhibit practical skills and the ability to solve real-world problems.

In education and professional settings, the importance of practical application cannot be overstated. While theoretical knowledge lays the foundation, it is the practical application that brings that knowledge to life, enabling individuals to understand, internalize, and leverage it effectively. Together, we will explore the significance of practical application, its benefits, and how it bridges the gap between theory and real-world success.

1. **Enhancing Understanding and Retention:** Practical application enhances understanding by allowing individuals to experience firsthand how theoretical concepts translate into real-world scenarios. Through hands-on experiences, individuals can bridge the gap between abstract theory and concrete application, making the knowledge more tangible and memorable. Practical application provides a context for learning, making it easier to retain and apply knowledge in future situations.

2. **Developing Critical Thinking and Problem-Solving Skills:** Practical application fosters critical thinking and

problem-solving skills. When individuals encounter real-world challenges, they must analyze, evaluate, and apply their knowledge to find solutions. This process encourages independent thinking, creative problem-solving, and adaptability. Practical application enables individuals to develop the ability to approach complex problems with confidence and resourcefulness.

3. **Building Competence and Skill Development:** Practical application is instrumental in building competence and developing practical skills. While theory provides the foundational knowledge, it is through practice that individuals gain proficiency and expertise. Whether it is in technical fields, creative arts, or professional disciplines, practical application allows individuals to refine their skills, improving their performance and increasing their value in the job market.

4. **Fostering Confidence and Self-Efficacy:** When individuals are given the opportunity to apply their theoretical knowledge in real-world situations, it boosts their confidence and self-efficacy. Successfully addressing challenges and achieving tangible results

validates their capabilities and strengthens their belief in their own abilities. This confidence and self-efficacy extend beyond the specific application and can positively impact their overall personal and professional growth.

5. **Bridging the Gap between Theory and Practice:** The gap between theory and practice is a common challenge, and practical application is the bridge that connects the two. Without practical application, theoretical knowledge may remain disconnected from its intended purpose, resulting in limited real-world impact. Practical application helps individuals understand how theory is relevant, applicable, and valuable in solving practical problems. It bridges the gap by demonstrating the direct connection between theory and real-world success.

6. **Improving Employability and Career Prospects:** Practical application plays a crucial role in enhancing employability and career prospects. Employers seek candidates who not only possess theoretical knowledge but also have the practical skills and experience to apply that knowledge

effectively. Practical application demonstrates an individual's ability to transfer theoretical concepts into real-world contexts, making them more desirable to prospective employers. It can also lead to valuable networking opportunities and recommendations from mentors or supervisors.

7. **Encouraging Continuous Learning:** Practical application fosters a mindset of continuous learning. As individuals apply their theoretical knowledge, they gain insights, identify gaps in their understanding, and uncover new areas for growth. This encourages them to seek further learning opportunities, whether through additional training, professional development programs, or advanced education. Practical application promotes lifelong learning, allowing individuals to stay relevant, adaptable, and competitive in a rapidly evolving world.

8. **Promoting Innovation and Creativity:** Practical application nurtures innovation and creativity. When individuals apply their theoretical knowledge, they are encouraged to think critically, challenge existing

assumptions, and seek novel solutions to problems. Practical application empowers individuals to experiment, take calculated risks, and explore new approaches. This fosters a culture of innovation within organizations and industries, driving progress and pushing boundaries.

9. **Building Resilience and Adaptability:** Practical application exposes individuals to the realities of the real world, including uncertainties, setbacks, and unexpected challenges. Through these experiences, individuals develop resilience and adaptability. They learn to navigate obstacles, adjust their approaches, and find alternative solutions. Practical application equips individuals with the skills to thrive in dynamic environments, where flexibility and the ability to embrace change are essential.

10. **Cultivating Ethical Decision-Making:** Practical application provides opportunities to engage with ethical dilemmas and make informed decisions. Applying theoretical knowledge in real-world contexts necessitates considering ethical implications and societal impact. Practical application fosters ethical decision-making by

challenging individuals to evaluate different perspectives, weigh consequences, and act responsibly. It cultivates a sense of ethics and social responsibility, shaping individuals into ethical leaders and responsible citizens.

Practical application is vital for bridging the gap between theory and real-world success. By enhancing understanding, developing critical thinking skills, building competence, fostering confidence, improving employability, promoting continuous learning, encouraging innovation, building resilience, and cultivating ethical decision-making, practical application empowers individuals to apply their theoretical knowledge effectively. It is through practical application that individuals develop the skills, competencies, and confidence needed to thrive in their personal and professional lives. Emphasizing the importance of practical application in educational and professional settings will lead to more impactful learning experiences, enhanced career prospects, and a stronger connection between theory and real-world success.

Developing Transferable Skills

One of the key ways to enhance the application of knowledge acquired through higher education is by focusing on the development of transferable skills. These are skills that can be applied across various industries and job roles, making individuals adaptable and versatile. Transferable skills include critical thinking, problem-solving, communication, teamwork, leadership, and adaptability. By consciously honing these skills, graduates can better navigate diverse work environments and demonstrate their value to employers.

In today's rapidly changing world, developing transferable skills has become essential for personal and professional success. Transferable skills, also known as soft skills or portable skills, are abilities that can be applied across various domains, industries, and roles. They enhance an individual's versatility, adaptability, and effectiveness in navigating diverse environments. Together, we will explore the importance of developing transferable skills, their benefits, and strategies for honing these valuable competencies.

1. **Adaptability:** Transferable skills enable individuals to adapt to different situations, environments, and demands. This adaptability is crucial in a world characterized by constant change and evolving work dynamics. Individuals with transferable skills can quickly acclimate to

new challenges, adjust their approaches, and embrace innovation.

2. **Communication:** Effective communication is a fundamental transferable skill that underpins success in all aspects of life. Strong verbal and written communication skills enable individuals to articulate ideas, collaborate with others, and convey information clearly and concisely. These skills foster productive teamwork, build relationships, and facilitate understanding across diverse audiences.

3. **Problem-Solving:** Transferable problem-solving skills empower individuals to identify, analyze, and resolve complex issues. These skills involve critical thinking, creativity, and resourcefulness. Problem-solving abilities allow individuals to navigate challenges, generate innovative solutions, and make informed decisions. This competency is highly sought after in today's dynamic and fast-paced work environments.

4. **Leadership:** Transferable leadership skills are valuable in various roles, not just managerial positions. Leadership skills involve inspiring and motivating others,

guiding teams, and facilitating collaboration. Strong leadership skills enable individuals to influence, inspire, and drive positive change within organizations and communities.

5. **Teamwork and Collaboration:** Effective teamwork and collaboration are critical in today's interconnected and diverse work environments. Transferable skills in this area involve fostering cooperation, active listening, conflict resolution, and the ability to work harmoniously with others towards shared goals. These skills enhance productivity, promote synergy, and contribute to a positive work culture.

6. **Time Management:** Transferable time management skills are essential for maximizing productivity and meeting deadlines. Individuals who possess these skills can prioritize tasks, organize their work efficiently, and optimize their time to achieve desired outcomes. Effective time management allows individuals to balance multiple responsibilities and maintain a healthy work-life integration.

7. **Flexibility:** Transferable skills encompass adaptability and flexibility. Individuals with

these skills are open to new ideas, approaches, and perspectives. They can readily adjust their strategies, embrace change, and thrive in dynamic work environments. Flexibility allows individuals to seize opportunities and navigate uncertainties with confidence.

8. **Emotional Intelligence:** Emotional intelligence is a crucial transferable skill that involves self-awareness, empathy, and the ability to manage emotions. Individuals with high emotional intelligence can navigate interpersonal relationships, demonstrate empathy, and respond appropriately to the emotions of others. This skill promotes effective communication, enhances teamwork, and fosters a positive work culture.

9. **Creativity and Innovation:** Transferable skills in creativity and innovation enable individuals to think outside the box, generate new ideas, and approach problems with fresh perspectives. These skills facilitate innovation, drive continuous improvement, and contribute to organizational growth and competitiveness.

10. **Critical Thinking:** Transferable critical thinking skills involve analyzing information, evaluating arguments, and making reasoned judgments. Individuals with strong critical thinking skills can assess complex situations, challenge assumptions, and arrive at well-informed decisions. This skill enhances problem-solving, strategic planning, and decision-making abilities.

11. **Resilience:** Resilience is a transferable skill that enables individuals to bounce back from setbacks, cope with adversity, and maintain a positive mindset. Resilient individuals can persevere in the face of challenges, learn from failures, and adapt to changing circumstances. This skill fosters personal growth, enhances problem-solving, and contributes to overall well-being.

12. **Networking:** Transferable networking skills involve building and nurturing professional relationships. Individuals with strong networking skills can connect with others, leverage their contacts, and create opportunities. Effective networking expands professional circles, facilitates career

development, and enhances the exchange of knowledge and resources.

13. **Cultural Competence:** Transferable cultural competence involves an understanding and appreciation of diverse cultures, perspectives, and experiences. This skill enables individuals to work effectively in multicultural environments, communicate across cultural boundaries, and demonstrate respect for different viewpoints. Cultural competence fosters inclusion, collaboration, and innovation.

14. **Ethics and Integrity:** Ethics and integrity are transferable skills that underpin ethical decision-making and responsible conduct. Individuals with strong ethical principles demonstrate honesty, trustworthiness, and accountability. These skills contribute to a positive work environment, build trust, and uphold ethical standards.

15. **Lifelong Learning:** Transferable skills encompass a mindset of lifelong learning. Individuals who embrace continuous learning can adapt to evolving technologies, industry trends, and changing skill requirements. This commitment to ongoing

development ensures professional growth, enables individuals to stay relevant, and enhances their career prospects.

Developing transferable skills is essential for personal and professional success in today's dynamic world. The versatility and adaptability offered by these skills allow individuals to navigate diverse environments, contribute effectively, and thrive in their chosen fields. The benefits of transferable skills extend beyond specific job roles, enabling individuals to seize opportunities, solve complex problems, and build meaningful relationships. By consciously developing these skills through learning opportunities, practice, and self-reflection, individuals can enhance their versatility, expand their career options, and embrace lifelong growth and success.

Internships and Work Experience

Internships and work experience are invaluable opportunities for college students and recent graduates to gain practical exposure in their chosen fields. Engaging in internships allows individuals to apply theoretical knowledge to real-world situations, develop industry-specific skills, and build professional networks. By actively seeking internships or part-time work during their studies or soon after graduation, individuals can bridge the gap between theory and practice and increase their employability.

Internships and work experience play a crucial role in shaping an individual's professional journey. They provide valuable opportunities for practical learning, skill development, and professional networking. Together, we will explore the significance of internships and work experience, the benefits they offer, and how they contribute to personal growth and career advancement.

1. **Bridging the Gap between Classroom and Workplace: Internships** and work experience provide a bridge between theoretical knowledge gained in classrooms and real-world applications. They allow individuals to apply their academic learning in practical settings, gaining hands-on experience and a deeper understanding of industry practices. This integration of theory and practice enhances the overall learning process, making it more relevant and meaningful.

2. **Skill Development:** Internships and work experience offer a platform for skill

development. They provide opportunities to hone industry-specific skills, such as technical expertise, project management, problem-solving, communication, teamwork, and leadership. Through practical application, individuals gain a deeper understanding of these skills and develop the proficiency necessary to succeed in their chosen field.

3. **Professional Networking:** Internships and work experience expose individuals to professional environments and facilitate networking opportunities. They provide direct access to professionals, mentors, and industry experts who can offer guidance, advice, and potential career opportunities. Building a strong professional network through internships and work experience can open doors for future employment, references, and collaborations.

4. **Industry Insights and Exposure:** Internships and work experience offer firsthand exposure to industry practices, trends, and challenges. Individuals get a chance to observe and engage with professionals in their field, witnessing the inner workings of organizations and gaining

insights into the industry's operations. This exposure helps individuals make informed career decisions, develop industry-specific knowledge, and understand the expectations and demands of the professional world.

5. **Resume Enhancement:** Internships and work experience significantly enhance resumes, making individuals more competitive in the job market. Employers often value candidates with practical experience, as it demonstrates their ability to apply knowledge, adapt to workplace dynamics, and contribute to organizational goals. Internships and work experience provide concrete examples of real-world achievements and responsibilities, making resumes more robust and compelling.

6. **Confidence Building:** Internships and work experience contribute to personal and professional confidence. By immersing themselves in practical settings, individuals gain a sense of accomplishment, develop self-assurance, and build confidence in their abilities. This confidence extends beyond specific tasks and roles, positively impacting future career endeavors and personal growth.

7. **Industry-Specific Knowledge:** Internships and work experience provide an opportunity to gain industry-specific knowledge that may not be covered extensively in academic programs. Moreover, to foundational knowledge, individuals acquire insights into industry trends, best practices, and emerging technologies. This industry-specific knowledge enhances their professional competency and positions them as valuable assets within their chosen field.

8. **Professional Etiquette and Workplace Skills:** Internships and work experience expose individuals to professional etiquette and workplace norms. They provide an opportunity to develop essential workplace skills, such as time management, communication, teamwork, and adaptability. Individuals learn to navigate office dynamics, handle responsibilities, and understand the expectations of employers, setting them up for success in future professional roles.

9. **Career Exploration and Clarification:** Internships and work experience allow individuals to explore different career paths and industries, helping them gain clarity

about their professional aspirations. They provide a firsthand understanding of various roles, allowing individuals to assess their compatibility with different job functions, work environments, and organizational cultures. This exploration helps individuals make informed decisions about their future career paths.

10. **Increased Employability:** Internships and work experience significantly enhance employability. Employers often prioritize candidates with relevant work experience, considering them to be more prepared for the demands of the job. Internships and work experience demonstrate an individual's commitment, initiative, and practical skills, making them attractive candidates in the competitive job market.

11. **Professional References and Mentoring:** Internships and work experience offer the opportunity to develop professional references and mentors. Positive recommendations from supervisors and mentors can significantly impact future career prospects. These references vouch for an individual's work ethic, skills, and

performance, enhancing their credibility and opening doors for future opportunities.

12. **Understanding Workplace Culture:** Internships and work experience provide insights into organizational cultures and dynamics. Individuals learn about the values, norms, and expectations within a specific workplace, preparing them for future work environments. This understanding enables individuals to adapt quickly, collaborate effectively, and navigate office politics with greater ease.

13. **Real-World Projects and Contributions:** Internships and work experience offer individuals the chance to work on real-world projects and contribute to organizational success. This practical involvement allows them to see the impact of their contributions, fostering a sense of purpose and fulfillment. The ability to showcase tangible accomplishments and contributions strengthens their professional profile and validates their capabilities.

14. **Personal Growth and Maturity:** Internships and work experience contribute to personal growth and maturity. By

navigating professional settings, individuals learn valuable life skills, including responsibility, independence, and resilience. They gain insights into their strengths and areas for improvement, fostering personal development and self-awareness.

15. **Transitioning to Full-Time Employment:** Internships and work experience often serve as stepping stones to full-time employment. Organizations frequently hire interns and individuals with relevant work experience, recognizing the value they bring to the team. Internships and work experience provide a smooth transition from academic life to the professional world, setting individuals on a path towards long-term career success.

Internships and work experience are invaluable opportunities for personal and professional growth. They bridge the gap between academic learning and real-world application, fostering skill development, professional networking, and industry-specific knowledge. By engaging in internships and work experience, individuals gain practical insights, enhance their employability, build confidence, and clarify their career goals. These experiences contribute to a well-rounded professional journey and pave the way for long-term success in the ever-evolving world of work.

Continuing Education and Professional Development

A college degree should be seen as a starting point rather than the end of one's educational journey. In today's rapidly evolving job market, it is crucial to engage in lifelong learning and stay updated with the latest industry trends and advancements. Pursuing continuing education, professional certifications, workshops, and online courses can provide individuals with the opportunity to acquire new skills, deepen their knowledge, and remain competitive in their respective fields.

Continuing education and professional development are essential components of a successful and fulfilling career. In a rapidly evolving world, individuals need to adapt, learn, and acquire new skills to stay relevant and meet the demands of their professions. Together, we will explore the significance of continuing education and professional development, the benefits they offer, and how they contribute to career growth and advancement.

1. Lifelong Learning Mindset: Continuing education and professional development cultivate a mindset of lifelong learning. They emphasize the importance of ongoing skill enhancement, knowledge acquisition, and personal growth throughout one's career. This mindset enables individuals to adapt to changing circumstances, embrace new technologies, and seize emerging opportunities.

2. Staying Current and Relevant: Continuing education ensures that professionals remain current and relevant in their respective fields. It enables individuals to stay abreast of the latest industry trends, advancements, and best practices. By updating their knowledge and skills, professionals can make informed decisions, contribute meaningfully to their organizations, and maintain their competitiveness in the job market.

3. Professional Networking: Continuing education and professional development programs offer opportunities for networking and building valuable connections. These platforms bring together like-minded professionals, subject matter experts, and industry leaders. Engaging in networking

activities allows individuals to exchange ideas, collaborate on projects, and foster mutually beneficial relationships that can lead to future career opportunities.

4. Skill Enhancement and Specialization: Continuing education enables professionals to enhance their existing skills and develop new ones. It offers specialized courses, workshops, and certifications that address specific areas of interest or emerging industry needs. Skill enhancement through continuing education enables professionals to diversify their expertise, pursue new career paths, and unlock higher levels of responsibility and leadership.

5. Career Advancement: Continuing education plays a vital role in career advancement. By acquiring new skills, knowledge, and certifications, professionals can position themselves for promotion or transition into higher-level roles. Employers often value candidates who invest in their professional development, recognizing their commitment to personal growth and their ability to contribute to organizational success.

6. Increased Employability: Continuing education enhances employability by expanding professionals' knowledge base and skill set. It demonstrates a proactive approach to learning and personal development, making individuals more attractive to prospective employers. Continually updating one's expertise through professional development activities ensures that professionals are well-equipped to meet the evolving demands of the job market.

7. Flexibility and Convenience: Continuing education programs offer flexibility and convenience, allowing professionals to pursue learning opportunities while balancing other commitments. Online courses, part-time programs, and self-paced learning options provide individuals with the flexibility to customize their learning journey based on their schedule and learning style. This accessibility encourages more professionals to engage in continuous learning.

8. Access to Expertise and Resources: Continuing education provides access to subject matter experts, thought leaders, and specialized resources. Professionals can learn

from industry veterans, gain insights into best practices, and access cutting-edge research and knowledge. This exposure to expertise and resources enhances professionals' problem-solving capabilities, decision-making skills, and overall competency.

9. Professional Recognition and Credibility: Engaging in continuing education and professional development activities boosts professional recognition and credibility. Earning certifications, attending workshops, or participating in industry conferences demonstrate a commitment to maintaining high standards of professionalism. These achievements not only provide validation of individuals' skills and knowledge but also enhance their reputation within their respective fields.

10. Innovation and Adaptability: Continuing education fosters innovation and adaptability. It exposes professionals to new ideas, emerging technologies, and industry trends. By staying informed about advancements in their fields, professionals can apply innovative solutions to complex problems, embrace change, and remain agile in their approach to work.

11. Personal Growth and Fulfillment: Continuing education contributes to personal growth and fulfillment. It allows professionals to explore their interests, pursue new passions, and expand their horizons beyond their current roles. Engaging in lifelong learning nurtures intellectual curiosity, boosts self-confidence, and provides a sense of accomplishment, leading to increased job satisfaction and overall well-being.

12. Professional Resilience: Continuing education builds professional resilience by equipping individuals with the skills and knowledge to navigate challenges and adapt to new circumstances. As industries evolve, professionals who have invested in continuous learning are better prepared to embrace change, upskill or reskill, and seize opportunities that arise during periods of transition.

13. Leadership Development: Continuing education supports leadership development by providing opportunities for professionals to enhance their leadership skills. Courses, workshops, and programs focused on leadership and management empower

professionals to inspire others, drive change, and lead with vision and integrity.

14. Global Perspective: Continuing education programs often foster a global perspective by promoting cross-cultural understanding and engagement. Professionals can engage with a diverse community of learners, share insights from different cultural contexts, and collaborate on projects with international participants. This exposure cultivates a broader worldview and prepares professionals for success in a globalized workforce.

15. Personal Branding and Differentiation: Continuing education allows professionals to differentiate themselves in a competitive job market. By acquiring specialized knowledge and certifications, professionals can build a unique personal brand and stand out from their peers. Continual learning demonstrates a commitment to professional growth and positions individuals as experts in their respective domains.

Continuing education and professional development are instrumental in nurturing lifelong learning, career growth, and personal fulfillment. They empower professionals to stay relevant, acquire new skills, network with industry peers, and adapt to changing work dynamics. By embracing continuous learning, professionals enhance their employability, expand their knowledge base, and unlock new opportunities for advancement. Investing in ongoing professional development is an investment in personal and career success in a rapidly evolving world.

Networking and Mentoring

Building a strong professional network and seeking guidance from mentors can significantly enhance the application of knowledge acquired during higher education. Networking allows individuals to connect with industry professionals, learn from their experiences, and gain insights into the practical aspects of their chosen fields. Mentors provide guidance, support, and valuable advice, helping individuals navigate their careers and make informed decisions. By actively networking and seeking mentorship, graduates can access valuable resources and opportunities for practical application.

Networking and mentoring are invaluable tools that can significantly impact an individual's personal and professional journey. Networking involves building relationships and connections with others, while mentoring involves receiving guidance and support from experienced individuals. Together, we will explore the power of networking and mentoring, their benefits, and how they contribute to personal and professional growth.

1. Expanding Opportunities: Networking opens doors to a world of opportunities. By connecting with a diverse range of professionals, individuals gain access to new career prospects, collaborations, partnerships, and industry insights. Networking enables individuals to expand their horizons, discover hidden opportunities, and uncover potential pathways for advancement.

2. Building Relationships: Networking allows individuals to build meaningful relationships with like-minded professionals. These relationships can lead to collaborations, referrals, and valuable partnerships. By fostering connections with individuals in similar fields or industries, individuals can

exchange ideas, support each other's growth, and create a strong support system.

3. Exchanging Knowledge and Insights: Networking provides a platform for the exchange of knowledge and insights. By engaging in conversations with professionals from different backgrounds and experiences, individuals gain diverse perspectives, ideas, and industry trends. This exposure to new information enhances individuals' understanding of their field and enables them to stay updated on the latest developments.

4. Enhancing Communication and Social Skills: Networking enhances communication and social skills. By regularly engaging with professionals, individuals refine their ability to articulate ideas, actively listen, and build rapport. These communication skills are crucial in professional settings, as they facilitate effective collaborations, negotiations, and presentations.

5. Professional Development: Networking contributes to professional development. By attending industry events, conferences, or seminars, individuals can participate in workshops, panel discussions, and

presentations that enhance their skills and knowledge. Networking events often feature thought leaders and experts who share their expertise, providing valuable learning opportunities for attendees.

6. Career Advancement: Networking plays a pivotal role in career advancement. Professionals who have a strong network often have access to insider information about job opportunities, promotions, and industry trends. Through their connections, they can receive recommendations, gain exposure to influential decision-makers, and position themselves for career growth.

7. Mentoring Support: Mentoring provides guidance, support, and advice from experienced professionals who have already walked a similar path. Mentors offer insights based on their own experiences, providing valuable perspectives, lessons learned, and practical advice. Mentoring relationships foster personal and professional growth, empowering individuals to navigate challenges and make informed decisions.

8. Knowledge Transfer: Mentoring enables the transfer of knowledge from experienced professionals to the next generation. Mentors share their expertise, skills, and industry-specific insights, empowering mentees to accelerate their learning curve and avoid common pitfalls. This knowledge transfer contributes to the development of well-rounded professionals who can make a meaningful impact in their fields.

9. Personal Growth: Mentoring facilitates personal growth. Through the guidance and support of a mentor, individuals gain self-confidence, clarity, and a sense of purpose. Mentoring relationships provide a safe space for mentees to explore their strengths, weaknesses, and aspirations, fostering self-awareness and personal development.

10. Expanded Network: Mentoring relationships often lead to expanded networks. Mentors, who are established professionals in their fields, can introduce mentees to their own network of contacts and provide valuable introductions. This expanded network opens doors to new connections, opportunities, and resources that can further support mentees' personal and professional growth.

11. Skill Enhancement: Mentoring contributes to skill enhancement. Mentors can identify areas where mentees need improvement and provide guidance on how to develop those skills. Whether it is leadership, communication, problem-solving, or technical skills, mentors offer insights and resources to help mentees strengthen their professional competencies.

12. Long-Term Support: Mentoring relationships often extend beyond specific projects or short-term goals. Mentors serve as long-term supporters, providing ongoing guidance and advice throughout an individual's career journey. This continuous support ensures that mentees have a trusted confidant and resource to rely on for advice, even as their careers evolve.

13. Inspiration and Motivation: Mentoring relationships can be a source of inspiration and motivation. Mentors, who have achieved success in their fields, serve as role models and demonstrate what is possible through hard work and dedication. Their stories of overcoming challenges and achieving

milestones inspire mentees to persevere and strive for their own goals.

14. Professional Identity and Branding: Mentoring relationships help individuals develop a professional identity and personal brand. Mentors can provide guidance on how to effectively communicate one's strengths, values, and unique contributions. This support helps mentees differentiate themselves in the job market and build a strong professional reputation.

15. Paying It Forward: Mentoring creates a culture of paying it forward. As mentees progress in their careers, they can become mentors themselves, passing on their knowledge, insights, and experiences to the next generation. This creates a ripple effect, nurturing a supportive and collaborative professional community.

Networking and mentoring are powerful tools that contribute to personal and professional growth. Networking expands opportunities, builds relationships, and fosters knowledge exchange. Mentoring provides guidance, support, and knowledge transfer from experienced professionals. By leveraging these resources, individuals can enhance their careers, expand their networks, gain valuable insights, and make a meaningful impact in their respective fields. Embracing networking and mentoring as integral parts of professional development ensures continuous growth, learning, and success in today's interconnected world.

Seeking Hands-On Learning Opportunities

Moreover, to internships, graduates can seek out hands-on learning opportunities such as volunteering, research projects, or involvement in community initiatives. These experiences offer practical application of knowledge, foster problem-solving skills, and provide exposure to different work environments. Engaging in hands-on learning allows individuals to gain valuable experience, demonstrate their abilities, and showcase their commitment to applying their knowledge effectively.

Hands-on learning opportunities offer individuals a unique and immersive educational experience that goes beyond traditional classroom settings. These experiential learning approaches provide practical, real-world experiences that bridge the gap between theory and application. Together, we will explore the value of seeking hands-on learning opportunities, the benefits they offer, and how they contribute to the acquisition of practical knowledge and skills.

1. Active Engagement and Immersion: Hands-on learning opportunities engage individuals actively in the learning process. Through direct involvement, individuals can immerse themselves in practical experiences, enabling a deeper understanding of concepts and principles. This active engagement facilitates the development of critical thinking, problem-solving, and decision-making skills in real-world scenarios.

2. Application of Theoretical Knowledge: Hands-on learning allows individuals to apply theoretical knowledge acquired in classrooms to practical situations. By putting concepts into practice, individuals gain a more comprehensive understanding of how theoretical ideas translate into tangible outcomes. This application of knowledge enhances retention, promotes deeper learning, and reinforces the relevance of academic concepts in real-world contexts.

3. Skill Development: Hands-on learning opportunities facilitate the development of a wide range of practical skills. Whether it is technical skills, communication skills, problem-solving skills, or teamwork skills, the hands-on approach allows individuals to practice and refine these competencies in authentic settings. This skill development enhances individuals' professional capabilities, making them more valuable in the job market.

4. Critical Thinking and Problem-Solving: Hands-on learning promote critical thinking and problem-solving abilities. By engaging in practical scenarios, individuals are confronted with real challenges that require analytical thinking, creativity, and adaptability. They learn to evaluate situations, identify problems, and devise effective solutions, honing their problem-solving skills in a dynamic and experiential manner.

5. Collaboration and Teamwork: Hands-on learning often involves collaborative projects or group activities, fostering teamwork and collaboration. Individuals learn to work effectively with others, leveraging collective

strengths and expertise to achieve common goals. This collaborative environment develops communication skills, conflict resolution abilities, and the ability to contribute to a team's success.

6. Building Confidence: Hands-on learning opportunities empower individuals, building confidence in their abilities. Through direct engagement, individuals gain firsthand experience, overcome challenges, and witness the impact of their actions. This sense of accomplishment fosters self-assurance, encouraging individuals to take on new challenges and pursue further learning opportunities with confidence.

7. Experiential Understanding: Hands-on learning provides an experiential understanding of concepts, phenomena, and processes. Instead of relying solely on abstract explanations, individuals can see and experience how theories manifest in practice. This experiential understanding deepens individuals' knowledge, allowing them to grasp the intricacies and complexities of real-world situations.

8. Adaptability and Resilience: Hands-on learning develops adaptability and resilience, preparing individuals for the dynamic and unpredictable nature of the professional world. By encountering unexpected challenges and uncertainties, individuals learn to adjust their approaches, think on their feet, and navigate complexities. This adaptability and resilience enable individuals to thrive in rapidly changing environments.

9. Real-World Networking Opportunities: Hands-on learning often provides networking opportunities with professionals, experts, and peers in relevant industries. Through internships, apprenticeships, or practical projects, individuals can connect with professionals in their field of interest. These networking opportunities can lead to mentorship, recommendations, and potential employment prospects, expanding individuals' professional networks.

10. Enhanced Employability: Hands-on learning experiences enhance individuals' employability. Employers often value candidates who have practical experience, as it demonstrates their ability to apply knowledge and skills effectively. Hands-on

learning allows individuals to showcase their capabilities, making them more competitive in the job market and increasing their chances of securing employment or internships.

11. Industry-Relevant Knowledge: Hands-on learning provides individuals with industry-relevant knowledge and insights. By engaging directly with professionals and experts, individuals gain exposure to current industry practices, trends, and emerging technologies. This industry-specific knowledge enhances individuals' marketability and ensures they are well-prepared to meet the demands of their chosen fields.

12. Professional Validation and Credentialing: Hands-on learning opportunities often offer professional validation and credentialing through certifications, licenses, or practical assessments. These credentials serve as tangible evidence of individuals' practical competence and expertise. They provide validation of individuals' skills and knowledge, enhancing their credibility and increasing their professional opportunities.

13. Personal Growth and Self-Discovery: Hands-on learning experiences promote personal growth and self-discovery. By actively engaging in practical activities, individuals gain insights into their strengths, interests, and areas for further development. They discover new passions, expand their horizons, and develop a deeper understanding of their own abilities and potential career paths.

14. Innovation and Creativity: Hands-on learning encourages innovation and creativity. Individuals are exposed to real-world challenges that require them to think creatively, explore alternative solutions, and embrace innovative approaches. This fosters an entrepreneurial mindset, inspiring individuals to become problem solvers and change agents in their chosen fields.

15. Lifelong Learning: Hands-on learning experiences instill a lifelong learning mindset. Individuals recognize that learning extends beyond formal education and that continuous growth and development are essential for career success. The hands-on approach encourages individuals to seek out new learning opportunities, embrace

emerging technologies, and adapt to evolving industry demands.

Seeking hands-on learning opportunities offers individuals a transformative educational experience. The active engagement, application of theoretical knowledge, skill development, critical thinking, collaboration, and personal growth fostered through hands-on learning contribute to well-rounded professionals who are equipped to excel in their chosen fields. By embracing practical experiences, individuals cultivate the necessary skills, knowledge, and confidence to thrive in the real world and make a meaningful impact in their personal and professional lives.

Embracing a Growth Mindset

A growth mindset is crucial for individuals looking to apply their college degree effectively. Embracing a growth mindset involves having a positive attitude towards learning, seeking challenges, accepting failure as an opportunity for growth, and embracing continuous improvement. By adopting this mindset, individuals are more likely to take risks, step out of their comfort zones, and apply their knowledge with confidence.

While earning a college degree is a significant accomplishment, its true value lies in the ability to apply the acquired knowledge effectively. Graduates must recognize the importance of bridging the gap between theory and practice, developing transferable skills, gaining practical experience, engaging in continuous learning, and building a professional network. By actively applying their knowledge, graduates can maximize the benefits of their college education, increase their employability, and achieve long-term professional success. Remember, a college degree is not a guarantee of success, but the effective application of knowledge is the key to unlocking its true potential.

Embracing a growth mindset is a transformative approach to personal and professional development. Coined by psychologist Carol Dweck, a growth mindset is the belief that intelligence, abilities, and skills can be developed through dedication, effort, and perseverance. In contrast, a fixed mindset assumes that abilities are fixed and unchangeable. Together, we will explore the importance of embracing a growth mindset, its benefits, and how it can unlock our potential and lead to success.

1. The Power of Belief: A growth mindset begins with the belief that our abilities can be developed. By recognizing that our intelligence and skills are not fixed, we open ourselves up to the possibilities of growth and improvement. This shift in mindset allows us to embrace challenges, learn from failures, and persist in the face of obstacles.

2. Embracing Challenges: A growth mindset encourages us to embrace challenges as opportunities for growth. Instead of shying away from difficult tasks, we approach them with enthusiasm and curiosity. Challenges become learning experiences that stretch our abilities and expand our knowledge. Through this process, we develop resilience, problem-solving skills, and a deeper understanding of our capabilities.

3. Persistence and Effort: Embracing a growth mindset compels us to put in consistent effort and persevere in the face of setbacks. We understand that success comes from hard work, practice, and dedication. Instead of viewing failure as a reflection of our abilities, we see it as an opportunity to learn and improve. This resilience fuels our motivation and propels us towards achieving our goals.

4. Continuous Learning: A growth mindset fosters a love for learning and a desire for continuous self-improvement. We see learning as a lifelong journey, and we actively seek out opportunities to expand our knowledge and skills. Whether it is through formal education, professional development, or self-directed learning, we embrace new challenges and acquire new knowledge to enhance our personal and professional growth.

5. Overcoming Self-Doubt: A growth mindset helps us overcome self-doubt and the fear of failure. Instead of allowing self-limiting beliefs to hold us back, we recognize that our abilities can be developed with effort and persistence. We learn to view setbacks as temporary and setbacks as opportunities for learning and growth. This shift in thinking empowers us to take risks, step outside our comfort zones, and pursue our goals with confidence.

6. Cultivating Resilience: Embracing a growth mindset cultivates resilience, enabling us to bounce back from setbacks and adapt to changing circumstances. We understand that

failures and setbacks are part of the learning process and do not define our abilities or potential. This resilience allows us to approach challenges with a positive attitude, learn from mistakes, and continue moving forward.

7. Embracing Feedback: A growth mindset encourages us to embrace feedback as a valuable tool for growth and improvement. Instead of viewing feedback as criticism, we see it as an opportunity to gain insights, learn from others, and refine our skills. We actively seek feedback and incorporate it into our personal and professional development, recognizing that it is a crucial component of our growth journey.

8. Nurturing Creativity and Innovation: A growth mindset nurtures creativity and innovation. When we believe that our abilities can be developed, we are more willing to explore new ideas, take risks, and think outside the box. We embrace challenges as opportunities to find unique solutions, fostering a culture of innovation and creativity in our personal and professional lives.

9. Building Resilient Relationships: A growth mindset extends to our relationships with others. We recognize that everyone has the potential for growth and development. By embracing a growth mindset, we support and encourage others in their own journeys, fostering a culture of collaboration, empathy, and shared growth. This mindset strengthens relationships, promotes teamwork, and creates a supportive and uplifting environment.

10. Increased Adaptability: Embracing a growth mindset enhances our adaptability to change. We understand that change is an opportunity for growth and learning, rather than a source of fear or resistance. With a growth mindset, we are more open to new ideas, flexible in our thinking, and willing to embrace new opportunities. This adaptability allows us to navigate uncertainty and thrive in dynamic environments.

11. Expanding Potential: A growth mindset expands our potential by challenging self-imposed limitations. By believing in our capacity for growth, we are more likely to explore new avenues, take on new roles, and pursue ambitious goals. This mindset unlocks

our untapped potential, enabling us to achieve levels of success that may have seemed unattainable with a fixed mindset.

12. Encouraging Collaboration and Learning from Others: A growth mindset fosters collaboration and a willingness to learn from others. We value diverse perspectives and recognize the opportunity for growth that comes from engaging with individuals who have different experiences and expertise. By embracing collaboration, we broaden our knowledge, challenge our assumptions, and enhance our problem-solving capabilities.

13. Reshaping Our Self-Identity: A growth mindset reshapes our self-identity by challenging limiting beliefs and negative self-perceptions. We see ourselves as capable of growth and improvement, which allows us to step into new roles, pursue new challenges, and redefine our personal and professional identities. This positive self-perception propels us to take risks and embrace opportunities for growth.

14. Embracing Innovation and Entrepreneurship: A growth mindset is closely linked to innovation and entrepreneurship. Individuals

with a growth mindset are more likely to identify opportunities, take calculated risks, and innovate in their respective fields. They are not afraid to challenge the status quo, experiment with new ideas, and adapt to market trends. This mindset creates a fertile ground for entrepreneurial endeavors and the pursuit of innovative solutions.

15. A Journey of Personal and Professional Growth: Embracing a growth mindset is a lifelong journey of personal and professional growth. It requires self-reflection, self-awareness, and a commitment to continuous learning and development. By embracing this mindset, we unlock our full potential, cultivate resilience, and achieve long-term success and fulfillment in all aspects of our lives.

Embracing a growth mindset is transformative, empowering us to unlock our potential, achieve success, and experience personal and professional growth. By believing in our capacity for growth, embracing challenges, persisting in the face of setbacks, and valuing continuous learning, we cultivate resilience, innovation, and adaptability. With a growth mindset, we can overcome self-limiting beliefs, take risks, and pursue our goals with confidence and enthusiasm. By embracing this mindset, we embark on a lifelong journey of growth and fulfillment, achieving success and making a meaningful impact in the world around us.

Emphasizing Experiential Learning

Incorporating experiential learning opportunities within the higher education curriculum can greatly enhance the application of knowledge. This can include internships, cooperative education programs, service-learning projects, and simulations. Experiential learning allows students to directly engage with real-world challenges, apply their knowledge in practical settings, and gain valuable insights and skills that cannot be attained through classroom instruction alone.

Encouraging Critical Thinking and Problem-Solving

Higher education institutions should prioritize the development of critical thinking and problem-solving skills. These skills are essential for effectively applying knowledge in complex situations and finding innovative solutions. Courses that promote analytical thinking, logical reasoning, and problem-solving methodologies can empower students to navigate uncertainties, evaluate information critically, and make informed decisions in professional settings.

Promoting Entrepreneurship and Innovation

Encouraging an entrepreneurial mindset among students can foster a proactive approach to applying their knowledge. Higher education institutions can offer entrepreneurship programs, innovation centers, and incubators to support aspiring entrepreneurs and innovators. These initiatives provide students with the tools and resources to apply their knowledge in entrepreneurial ventures, drive innovation, and create value in the marketplace.

Collaborative and Interdisciplinary Learning

Promoting collaborative and interdisciplinary learning environments can enhance the application of knowledge by fostering teamwork, communication, and the ability to integrate diverse perspectives. Group projects, interdisciplinary courses, and collaborative research opportunities enable students to work together on complex problems, leverage their collective knowledge, and develop practical solutions that draw from various disciplines.

Encouraging Reflective Practice

Engaging in reflective practice allows individuals to consciously reflect on their learning experiences, connect theory to practice, and identify areas for growth and improvement. Higher education institutions can encourage students to engage in self-reflection through journaling, portfolio development, or guided reflection exercises. By reflecting on their experiences, students can deepen their understanding of how to apply knowledge effectively and refine their skills over time.

Cultivating Professional Skills

Moreover, to subject-specific knowledge, higher education should place emphasis on cultivating essential professional skills. These skills include communication, leadership, teamwork, adaptability, and ethical decision-making. By integrating professional skill development into the curriculum, students can effectively apply their knowledge in professional settings and demonstrate the competencies sought by employers.

Engaging with Industry Partners

Establishing strong partnerships with industry organizations and professionals can provide students with valuable insights into the practical applications of their knowledge. Guest lectures, industry panels, and collaborative projects with industry partners can expose students to real-world challenges, industry best practices, and the latest trends. Such collaborations bridge the gap between academia and industry, allowing students to apply their knowledge in relevant contexts and establish connections that can lead to future employment opportunities.

Continuous Feedback and Assessment

Higher education institutions should adopt a culture of continuous feedback and assessment to help students gauge their progress and identify areas for improvement. Formative assessments, peer evaluations, and constructive feedback from professors can guide students in effectively applying their knowledge and developing their professional skills. Regular feedback also encourages students to reflect on their learning experiences, make necessary adjustments, and refine their application of knowledge over time.

The effective application of knowledge acquired through higher education requires a holistic approach that goes beyond classroom instruction. By incorporating experiential learning, promoting critical thinking and problem-solving, encouraging entrepreneurship and innovation, fostering collaboration and interdisciplinary learning, cultivating professional skills, engaging with industry partners, encouraging reflective practice, and providing continuous feedback and assessment, higher education institutions can equip students with the tools and experiences necessary to excel in applying their knowledge in real-world settings. This comprehensive approach prepares graduates to navigate the complexities of the professional world and maximize the benefits of their education.

CHAPTER THREE

Moving Away from Poverty

Escaping the clutches of poverty is a deeply transformative journey that encompasses both physical and mental liberation. Poverty, characterized by a lack of resources and opportunities, affects individuals on multiple levels, often perpetuating cycles of disadvantage. However, by addressing the physical and mental aspects of poverty, individuals can break free from its grip and create a path towards a brighter future. This book explores the importance of both physical and mental liberation in moving away from poverty and highlights the strategies and mindset needed to embark on this transformative journey.

1. Understanding the Multi-dimensional Nature of Poverty: Poverty is not solely an economic condition; it affects individuals physically, mentally, and emotionally. Physical poverty manifests as a lack of basic necessities, such as food, shelter, and healthcare, while mental poverty encompasses limited access to education, opportunities, and the belief in one's abilities. Recognizing the multi-

dimensional nature of poverty is crucial to addressing its root causes and working towards sustainable change.

2. Addressing Physical Poverty: Physical poverty can be addressed by providing access to basic needs and resources. This includes initiatives such as affordable housing, healthcare services, nutrition programs, and infrastructure development. By ensuring that individuals have their fundamental physical needs met, the cycle of poverty can be interrupted, allowing individuals to focus on their personal and professional growth.

3. Enhancing Education and Skill Development: Education is a powerful tool for mental liberation. By providing quality education and skill development opportunities, individuals can acquire the knowledge and abilities necessary to secure employment, start businesses, and break free from the limitations of poverty. Accessible and inclusive education systems play a crucial role in equipping individuals with the skills they need to succeed and thrive.

4. Fostering Financial Literacy and Entrepreneurship: Financial literacy is key to breaking the cycle of poverty. By providing individuals with the knowledge and skills to manage their finances effectively, they can make informed decisions, save, invest, and plan for the future. Entrepreneurship also plays a vital role in economic empowerment, as it enables individuals to create their own opportunities and generate income. By fostering a culture of financial literacy and entrepreneurship, individuals can move away from poverty and build sustainable livelihoods.

5. Cultivating Resilience and a Growth Mindset: Mental liberation from poverty involves cultivating resilience and developing a growth mindset. Resilience enables individuals to bounce back from setbacks, persevere in the face of challenges, and maintain a positive outlook. A growth mindset encourages individuals to believe in their ability to learn, grow, and overcome obstacles. By cultivating these qualities, individuals can navigate the complexities of poverty, seize opportunities, and create a better future for themselves and their families.

6. Breaking the Chains of Generational Poverty: Generational poverty can be a deeply ingrained cycle that persists across multiple generations. Breaking free from this cycle requires addressing both physical and mental aspects. It involves providing children with access to quality education, nurturing their talents and abilities, and instilling in them a sense of hope and ambition. By equipping future generations with the tools and opportunities to thrive, the cycle of poverty can be broken, and families can build a legacy of prosperity.

7. Community Empowerment and Collaboration: Moving away from poverty requires collective action and community empowerment. Building strong social networks, fostering collaboration, and advocating for systemic change are vital components of the journey. Communities can come together to create support systems, provide mentorship, and advocate for policies that promote equal access to opportunities. By working collectively, individuals can amplify their impact and create lasting change.

8. Access to Healthcare and Mental Well-being: Physical and mental well-being are interconnected. Access to affordable healthcare services, including mental health support, is crucial in addressing the mental impact of poverty. By ensuring access to healthcare and promoting mental well-being, individuals can overcome the psychological burdens of poverty and improve their overall quality of life.

Moving away from poverty physically and mentally requires a comprehensive approach that addresses both the physical conditions and the mental barriers that perpetuate poverty. By addressing physical poverty through access to basic needs and resources, enhancing education and skill development, fostering financial literacy and entrepreneurship, cultivating resilience and a growth mindset, breaking generational poverty, fostering community empowerment, and promoting access to healthcare and mental well-being, individuals can embark on a transformative journey towards liberation. By empowering individuals to take control of their lives and providing them with the tools and opportunities to thrive, we can build a society where poverty is no longer an insurmountable obstacle, but a challenge that can be overcome with determination, support, and collective action.

Tired of Being Broke and In Need?

Being broke is a challenging and disheartening experience that many people strive to overcome. It brings financial stress, limited opportunities, and a sense of helplessness. Higher education can play a significant role in breaking free from the cycle of poverty and transforming one's financial situation. This book explores the impact of higher education on escaping financial struggles, highlighting the importance of personal growth, expanded career opportunities, financial literacy, and the development of transferable skills.

Gaining higher education training offers numerous benefits that contribute to moving away from financial struggles. It cultivates personal growth, expands career opportunities, enhances financial literacy, and fosters the development of transferable skills. Through higher education, individuals gain access to professional networks, resources, and support systems that propel them toward financial stability. Moreover, higher education promotes lifelong learning, critical thinking, and adaptability, essential qualities for success in a rapidly changing world. By embracing the opportunities provided by higher education, individuals can pave their own path toward financial prosperity, personal fulfillment, and a brighter future.

1. Understanding the Discomfort of Being Broke: Being broke is a difficult and uncomfortable state. It hampers one's ability to meet basic needs, pursue dreams, and enjoy a sense of security. The constant worry about finances and limited access to resources can lead to feelings of frustration and hopelessness. Recognizing the discomfort of being broke becomes a powerful catalyst for seeking change and embracing higher education as a means to escape this situation.

2. Empowering Personal Growth: Higher education offers an environment for personal growth and self-improvement. Through academic pursuits, students gain knowledge, broaden their perspectives, and develop critical thinking skills. Education expands horizons, instills confidence, and fosters a sense of purpose. By engaging in higher education, individuals can develop the mindset, knowledge, and skills necessary to

overcome financial struggles and build a more secure future.

3. Opening Doors to Expanded Career Opportunities: One of the key advantages of higher education is the access it provides to a wider range of career opportunities. By acquiring specialized knowledge and qualifications, individuals become eligible for higher-paying jobs in fields that require advanced education. Higher education equips individuals with the necessary expertise and credentials to pursue careers with greater earning potential, offering a pathway out of financial struggles.

4. Enhancing Financial Literacy: Higher education promotes financial literacy, which is crucial for managing personal finances effectively. By studying subjects such as economics, accounting, or personal finance, individuals gain a deeper understanding of budgeting, investments, and debt management. Financial literacy empowers individuals to make informed decisions, avoid financial pitfalls, and plan for their long-term financial well-being. It equips them with the tools to break free from the cycle of living paycheck to paycheck.

5. Developing Transferable Skills: Higher education equips individuals with a broad range of transferable skills that are highly valued in the job market. These skills, such as critical thinking, communication, problem-solving, and teamwork, are applicable across various industries and job roles. By developing these skills, individuals enhance their employability and increase their chances of securing well-paying positions. This ultimately leads to improved financial stability and a reduced likelihood of being broke.

6. Networking and Mentorship: Higher education institutions provide opportunities for networking and mentorship, which are instrumental in career development and financial success. Building connections with professors, peers, and industry professionals opens doors to job prospects, internships, and mentorship relationships. Mentors can provide guidance, advice, and support, sharing their expertise and helping individuals navigate their career paths. Networking and mentorship create a supportive ecosystem that enhances

professional growth and increases the chances of financial stability.

7. Access to Scholarships and Financial Aid: Higher education offers access to scholarships, grants, and financial aid programs that can significantly reduce the financial burden of pursuing education. These resources make higher education more attainable for individuals from low-income backgrounds. By leveraging scholarships and financial aid, individuals can pursue their educational goals without accumulating excessive debt, setting a solid foundation for financial stability and success.

8. Fostering an Entrepreneurial Mindset: Higher education nurtures an entrepreneurial mindset, encouraging individuals to think creatively, take calculated risks, and seize opportunities. Entrepreneurship provides an alternative path to financial success, allowing individuals to create their own businesses and generate income on their terms. Higher education equips individuals with the knowledge and skills needed to start and manage successful ventures, empowering them to escape the cycle of financial struggles.

9. Developing a Strong Work Ethic: Higher education instills a strong work ethic in individuals. The rigorous academic demands, deadlines, and assignments require discipline and dedication. By cultivating a strong work ethic, individuals are better prepared to enter the workforce and take on the challenges that come with it. This commitment to hard work translates into improved job performance, career advancement, and increased earning potential, helping individuals move away from financial struggles.

10. Access to Professional Development Opportunities: Higher education institutions often provide access to professional development opportunities, such as workshops, seminars, and internships. These experiences allow students to gain practical skills, industry-specific knowledge, and exposure to professional environments. Engaging in professional development activities enhances individuals' employability, making them more attractive to employers and increasing their chances of securing higher-paying positions.

11. Cultivating Financial Discipline: Higher education emphasizes the importance of financial discipline and responsible money management. Through courses or workshops on personal finance, individuals learn about budgeting, saving, and investing. They acquire the tools and knowledge to make sound financial decisions, avoid unnecessary debt, and build a strong financial foundation. This financial discipline becomes a key component of moving away from financial struggles and achieving long-term financial stability.

12. Increased Job Security: Higher education provides individuals with increased job security. In a competitive job market, employers often prioritize candidates with higher education qualifications. Having a degree or specialized training gives individuals a competitive edge and enhances their marketability. With a stable and secure job, individuals can more effectively plan for their financial future, reduce financial stress, and gain a sense of stability and control over their lives.

13. Access to Advanced Technology and Resources: Higher education institutions offer access to advanced technology, research facilities, libraries, and other resources that individuals may not have access to otherwise. These resources facilitate learning, skill development, and innovation. By leveraging these tools, individuals can stay current with industry trends, gain practical experience with modern technologies, and position themselves as valuable assets in their chosen fields.

14. Exposure to Diverse Perspectives: Higher education exposes individuals to a diverse range of perspectives, cultures, and ideas. Interacting with a diverse student body and faculty fosters cultural competence, empathy, and a broader understanding of the world. This exposure enhances individuals' ability to navigate diverse work environments, collaborate effectively, and seize opportunities in a globalized economy. It also cultivates a mindset of inclusivity and adaptability, which are essential for personal and professional growth.

15. Lifelong Learning and Adaptability: Higher education promotes a lifelong learning mindset, encouraging individuals to continue acquiring knowledge and developing new skills even after graduation. This mindset of continuous learning and adaptability is crucial in a rapidly evolving job market. By embracing lifelong learning, individuals can remain competitive, adapt to changing circumstances, and stay ahead of industry trends, ensuring long-term career success and financial stability.

16. Access to Supportive Alumni Networks: Higher education institutions often have extensive alumni networks that offer ongoing support, mentorship, and career guidance. Alumni associations provide opportunities for networking, job referrals, and professional development events. Being part of such networks connects individuals to a community of like-minded professionals who can offer guidance and support throughout their careers, further enhancing their chances of financial success.

17. Improved Social Mobility: Higher education serves as a vehicle for social mobility, allowing individuals to transcend their socio-economic backgrounds. It provides opportunities for individuals from disadvantaged communities to access resources, develop skills, and break free from the limitations imposed by their circumstances. Higher education levels the playing field, offering a pathway for upward mobility and empowering individuals to achieve financial independence and improve their quality of life.

18. Enhanced Critical Thinking and Problem-Solving Abilities: Higher education sharpens critical thinking and problem-solving abilities. Through rigorous coursework, individuals develop analytical skills, the ability to evaluate information critically, and solve complex problems. These skills are invaluable in the workplace, where individuals are required to make informed decisions, assess risks, and develop innovative solutions. Strong critical thinking and problem-solving abilities contribute to professional growth, career advancement, and increased earning potential.

19. Access to Research and Innovation: Higher education institutions are hubs for research and innovation. Students have the opportunity to engage in research projects, contribute to knowledge creation, and make meaningful discoveries. This exposure to research fosters a spirit of innovation, entrepreneurship, and creative thinking. Individuals who harness these skills and pursue entrepreneurial endeavors have the potential to create innovative solutions, launch successful businesses, and achieve financial prosperity.

20. Personal Fulfillment and Confidence: Lastly, higher education offers personal fulfillment and boosts self-confidence. Accomplishing educational milestones and acquiring knowledge in a chosen field instills a sense of pride and confidence in one's abilities. This newfound confidence translates into increased self-belief, assertiveness, and resilience. Individuals who are confident in their skills and knowledge are more likely to pursue higher-paying opportunities, negotiate better salaries, and take calculated risks that lead to financial success.

Escaping the grip of financial struggles is an aspirational goal for many individuals. Higher education serves as a powerful vehicle for achieving this objective, offering personal growth, expanded career opportunities, financial literacy, transferable skills, networking, mentorship, access to scholarships and financial aid, and an entrepreneurial mindset. By embracing higher education, individuals can equip themselves with the necessary tools to break free from financial limitations, achieve financial stability, and build a brighter future. It is through higher education that individuals can pave the way for personal growth, professional success, and the enjoyment of financial well-being, ultimately leaving the challenges of being broke behind.

Thirst for Economic and Financial Change

In a world marked by economic disparities and financial challenges, there is a growing thirst for change. People are seeking a transformation that can uplift communities, bridge inequalities, and create a more equitable and prosperous society. This book examines the reasons behind this thirst for economic and financial change and explores how collective action, policy reforms, innovation, and inclusive growth can pave the way for a brighter future.

The thirst for economic and financial change is a call to action, urging us to create a society where opportunities, resources, and wealth are distributed equitably. By embracing inclusive growth, reducing income inequality, enhancing financial literacy, investing in education, promoting sustainable development, fostering entrepreneurship and innovation, strengthening social safety nets, encouraging ethical business practices, and embracing technology, we can quench this thirst for change. It is through collective efforts, policy reforms, and a commitment to fairness and justice that we can create a future where economic and financial systems work for the betterment of all. Let us embark on this journey of transformation and create a world where economic and financial change becomes a reality, ensuring a brighter and more prosperous future for generations to come.

1. Recognizing the Inequities: The first step in addressing the thirst for economic and financial change is recognizing the inequities that exist. It is essential to acknowledge the disparities in wealth distribution, access to resources, and opportunities that perpetuate inequality. By acknowledging these realities,

we can develop a shared understanding of the urgent need for change.

2. Embracing Inclusive Growth: Economic and financial change must prioritize inclusive growth that benefits all members of society, regardless of their socio-economic background. Inclusive growth ensures that everyone has access to quality education, healthcare, and job opportunities. It aims to bridge the gap between the rich and the poor, empowering marginalized communities and fostering social mobility.

3. Reducing Income Inequality: Addressing income inequality is a crucial aspect of economic and financial change. It involves creating policies and programs that redistribute wealth, promote fair wages, and ensure that the benefits of economic growth are shared equitably. By narrowing the income gap, we can create a more balanced and sustainable economy that benefits society as a whole.

4. Enhancing Financial Literacy: Improving financial literacy is key to fostering economic and financial change. By equipping individuals with the knowledge and skills

needed to manage their finances effectively, we can empower them to make informed decisions, avoid debt traps, and build wealth. Financial literacy programs should be accessible to all, providing individuals with the tools to navigate the complexities of the financial world.

5. Investing in Education: Investing in education is an investment in economic and financial change. By ensuring access to quality education from early childhood to higher education, we can equip individuals with the knowledge and skills needed to compete in the global economy. Education provides the foundation for innovation, entrepreneurship, and critical thinking, fostering economic growth and social progress.

6. Promoting Sustainable Development: Economic and financial change should be guided by the principles of sustainable development. This involves integrating environmental, social, and economic considerations into decision-making processes. Sustainable development recognizes the interconnectedness of economic growth, environmental

conservation, and social well-being. By adopting sustainable practices, we can create a resilient and inclusive economy that safeguards our planet for future generations.

7. Fostering Entrepreneurship and Innovation: Entrepreneurship and innovation are powerful drivers of economic and financial change. They create jobs, stimulate economic growth, and drive technological advancements. Supporting aspiring entrepreneurs, providing access to capital, and creating an enabling environment for innovation can unleash the transformative power of entrepreneurship, fostering economic and financial change.

8. Strengthening Social Safety Nets: Creating robust social safety nets is essential to address economic and financial vulnerabilities. Safety nets, such as unemployment benefits, healthcare coverage, and social assistance programs, provide a lifeline for those facing economic hardships. By strengthening and expanding social safety nets, we can protect individuals and families from the adverse effects of economic shocks, promoting stability and resilience.

9. Encouraging Ethical and Responsible Business Practices: Economic and financial change should be underpinned by ethical and responsible business practices. This involves promoting transparency, accountability, and corporate social responsibility. Businesses play a vital role in shaping the economy and society, and by aligning their practices with ethical standards, they can contribute to a more sustainable and equitable economic system.

10. Embracing Technology and Digital Transformation: Technology and digital transformation have the potential to revolutionize economies and drive economic and financial change. Embracing technological advancements, promoting digital literacy, and fostering an environment conducive to innovation can unlock new opportunities, create jobs, and enhance productivity. It is crucial to ensure that the benefits of technological advancements are accessible to all, including marginalized communities.

The Myths about Higher Education

Higher education has long been regarded as a transformative journey, equipping individuals with knowledge, skills, and opportunities for personal and professional growth. However, alongside the benefits, several myths have emerged surrounding higher education, often leading to misconceptions and misunderstandings. This book aims to debunk some of these myths, shedding light on the true value and significance of higher education in today's society.

Higher education plays a pivotal role in shaping individuals' lives, providing them with knowledge, skills, and opportunities for personal and professional growth. However, misconceptions and myths surrounding higher education often cloud its true value and impact. Together, we will refute common myths surrounding higher education, highlighting the transformative power it holds and its relevance in today's society.

1. **Myth:** Higher Education Guarantees Immediate Success and Wealth: One common myth is that obtaining a higher education degree guarantees immediate success and wealth. While higher education provides individuals with a competitive

advantage in the job market, it is not a guarantee of instant financial prosperity. Success and wealth are influenced by various factors, including market conditions, individual effort, and external opportunities. Higher education serves as a foundation for long-term career growth and economic stability, but success ultimately relies on additional factors such as work ethic, experience, and networking.

2. **Myth:** College is Only for Academically Inclined Individuals: Another myth is that college is exclusively for academically inclined individuals. This misconception overlooks the diverse range of programs and career paths available within higher education. Colleges and universities offer programs in fields such as trade skills, vocational training, arts, sports, and entrepreneurship. Higher education accommodates different learning styles and interests, providing opportunities for individuals with various talents and aspirations to excel in their chosen fields.

3. **Myth:** College Degrees Are Becoming Irrelevant in the Digital Age: With the rise of technology and the emphasis on skills-based

learning, some argue that traditional college degrees are becoming irrelevant in the digital age. However, this is a myth. While the digital age has brought about new opportunities for acquiring knowledge and skills, college degrees continue to hold value. Higher education equips individuals with critical thinking abilities, communication skills, and a broader understanding of the world, which are essential in navigating complex societal challenges and adapting to evolving career landscapes.

4. **Myth:** Higher Education is a One-Size-Fits-All Approach: Another myth is that higher education follows a one-size-fits-all approach. In reality, higher education offers a multitude of pathways and options tailored to individual interests and career goals. From community colleges to trade schools, technical institutes to four-year universities, individuals have the flexibility to choose an educational path that aligns with their unique aspirations and circumstances. Higher education is a dynamic and diverse ecosystem, accommodating a wide range of learning styles, career trajectories, and personal preferences.

5. **Myth:** College Graduates Will Always Secure Higher-Paying Jobs: A prevailing myth is that college graduates will always secure higher-paying jobs compared to those without a degree. While higher education can increase earning potential, it does not guarantee automatic financial success. The job market is influenced by various factors, including industry trends, market demand, and individual skills. Furthermore, the value of a degree may vary depending on the field of study, location, and personal factors. Higher education serves as a foundation, but individuals must continue to develop skills, gain experience, and adapt to the demands of the job market.

6. **Myth:** Higher Education is Exclusively for Young Individuals: There is a myth that higher education is exclusively for young individuals fresh out of high school. However, higher education caters to learners of all ages and backgrounds. Many colleges and universities offer programs specifically designed for adult learners, working professionals, and individuals seeking career transitions. Lifelong learning is encouraged, and higher education institutions provide

opportunities for individuals to acquire new skills and knowledge throughout their lives.

7. **Myth:** Higher Education is an Unaffordable Financial Burden: One prevalent myth is that higher education is an unaffordable financial burden. While the cost of higher education is a concern for many, financial assistance options such as scholarships, grants, and student loans are available to help individuals finance their education. Furthermore, community colleges and trade schools often offer more affordable alternatives to traditional universities. It is important to explore all available options, including financial aid, to make higher education more accessible and manageable.

8. **Myth:** Practical Skills Trump Theoretical Knowledge: A common myth suggests that practical skills are more valuable than theoretical knowledge gained through higher education. While practical skills are undoubtedly important, higher education offers a balanced approach that combines theoretical understanding with practical application. Theoretical knowledge forms the foundation for critical thinking, problem-solving, and adaptability, while practical

skills enable individuals to apply their knowledge effectively in real-world contexts. Both theoretical knowledge and practical skills are complementary and contribute to well-rounded professionals.

Debunking the myths surrounding higher education is crucial for understanding its true value and significance in today's society. Higher education provides individuals with a range of benefits, including career opportunities, personal growth, critical thinking abilities, and a broader understanding of the world. It accommodates diverse interests and career paths, caters to learners of all ages, and offers various financial assistance options. By dispelling these myths, we can appreciate the transformative power of higher education and the opportunities it provides for individuals to thrive and contribute to their communities and society at large.

By refuting the myths surrounding higher education, we can recognize its true value and dispel misconceptions. Higher education provides individuals with the knowledge, skills, and opportunities necessary for personal growth, professional success, and societal advancement. It is not a one-size-fits-all approach but offers diverse pathways tailored to individual interests and career goals. Higher education equips individuals with theoretical knowledge, practical skills, critical thinking abilities, and adaptability, preparing them to thrive in a dynamic and ever-evolving world. By embracing the transformative power of higher education, we can unlock new possibilities and create a more enlightened and prosperous society.

CHAPTER FOUR

Famous Believers About Higher Education

Higher education has been championed by numerous famous individuals from various fields who recognize its value in personal growth, intellectual development, and societal progress. Here are a few examples of famous people who have expressed support for higher education:

1. Barack Obama: The 44th President of the United States, Barack Obama, has consistently emphasized the importance of higher education. During his presidency, he launched the "Educate to Innovate" campaign, promoting science, technology, engineering, and mathematics (STEM) education. He also emphasized the need to make higher education more accessible and affordable, advocating for initiatives such as the Pell Grant program and the expansion of community college programs.

2. Malala Yousafzai: Nobel Peace Prize laureate and education activist, Malala Yousafzai, is a strong advocate for the right

to education. After surviving an assassination attempt by the Taliban for speaking out about girls' education, she became a global symbol of the fight for education equality. Yousafzai has consistently highlighted the transformative power of education, particularly for marginalized communities and girls worldwide.

3. Michelle Obama: Former First Lady Michelle Obama has been a vocal advocate for higher education, particularly for underprivileged and minority students. Through initiatives like "Reach Higher" and "Better Make Room," she has encouraged students to pursue higher education, provided resources for college preparation, and advocated for college affordability and accessibility.

4. Elon Musk: Entrepreneur and business magnate Elon Musk, known for his ventures such as SpaceX and Tesla, has stressed the importance of higher education in fostering critical thinking and innovation. While he himself dropped out of Stanford University, Musk has expressed the value of higher education in developing foundational

knowledge and skills necessary for success in technical fields.

5. Oprah Winfrey: Media mogul and philanthropist Oprah Winfrey has emphasized the transformative power of education throughout her career. Through the Oprah Winfrey Foundation, she has supported various educational initiatives, including scholarships and the creation of educational programs. Winfrey has consistently highlighted education as a means of empowerment and personal growth.

6. Bill Gates: Co-founder of Microsoft and philanthropist Bill Gates is a strong proponent of higher education. Through the Bill & Melinda Gates Foundation, he has invested significantly in educational initiatives, particularly in improving educational access and quality. Gates has emphasized the role of higher education in addressing global challenges and fostering innovation.

7. Sheryl Sandberg: Chief Operating Officer of Facebook and author of "Lean In," Sheryl Sandberg has advocated for women's empowerment and leadership in the

workplace. She has highlighted the importance of higher education in providing women with the necessary skills, knowledge, and confidence to succeed in their careers.

8. Nelson Mandela: The late Nelson Mandela, the former President of South Africa and renowned anti-apartheid leader, believed in the power of education to break the cycle of poverty and inequality. Mandela famously stated, "Education is the most powerful weapon which you can use to change the world." He understood that education equips individuals with the tools to challenge injustice, develop critical thinking, and contribute positively to society.

9. Angela Merkel: Angela Merkel, the Chancellor of Germany and one of the world's most influential leaders, has consistently emphasized the importance of higher education and scientific research. Merkel, who holds a doctorate in physics, has emphasized the role of education and research in driving innovation, economic growth, and social progress. She has championed initiatives to increase funding for education and support scientific advancements.

10. Condoleezza Rice: Former U.S. Secretary of State Condoleezza Rice is a strong proponent of higher education. She has spoken about the transformative impact her education had on her life and career, emphasizing the importance of learning and intellectual curiosity. Rice has stressed the value of education in shaping critical thinking, expanding perspectives, and fostering global understanding.

11. Kofi Annan: The late Kofi Annan, former Secretary-General of the United Nations, believed in the power of education to promote peace, sustainable development, and global cooperation. He emphasized the importance of education in addressing the world's most pressing challenges, including poverty, conflict, and inequality. Annan advocated for educational opportunities for all, highlighting the role of education in nurturing responsible global citizens.

12. Indra Nooyi: Indra Nooyi, former CEO of PepsiCo, has spoken about the value of education and continuous learning throughout her career. She credits her education and the knowledge she gained for

her success in the business world. Nooyi has encouraged individuals to embrace lifelong learning, highlighting the role of education in building resilience, adaptability, and a foundation for professional growth.

13. Tim Cook: CEO of Apple Inc., Tim Cook has emphasized the importance of education in fostering innovation and driving technological advancements.

14. J.K. Rowling: The author of the Harry Potter series, J.K. Rowling has highlighted the transformative power of education and the role it played in her own journey.

15. Michelle Bachelet: Former President of Chile and United Nations High Commissioner for Human Rights, Michelle Bachelet has advocated for inclusive and accessible higher education opportunities for all.

16. Michael Bloomberg: Entrepreneur and philanthropist Michael Bloomberg has made significant contributions to higher education, supporting scholarships, research, and educational institutions.

17. Amal Clooney: Human rights lawyer Amal Clooney has emphasized the importance of education in promoting justice, equality, and human rights.

18. Bill Clinton: Former U.S. President Bill Clinton has promoted the value of higher education and its potential to improve individuals' lives and society as a whole.

19. Ruth Bader Ginsburg: The late Supreme Court Justice Ruth Bader Ginsburg believed in the power of education to promote equality and justice.

20. Warren Buffett: Business magnate and philanthropist Warren Buffett has emphasized the importance of investing in education to create a strong and prosperous society.

21. Shonda Rhimes: Television producer and writer Shonda Rhimes has spoken about the importance of education and its role in her own successful career.

22. Serena Williams: Tennis champion Serena Williams has encouraged young people to

pursue higher education, recognizing its value beyond sports achievements.

23. Lin-Manuel Miranda: Playwright and composer Lin-Manuel Miranda has highlighted the transformative power of education in fostering creativity and self-expression.

24. Satya Nadella: CEO of Microsoft, Satya Nadella has emphasized the need for continuous learning and the role of higher education in preparing individuals for the future.

25. Ellen DeGeneres: Television host and comedian Ellen DeGeneres has encouraged her viewers to pursue education and embrace lifelong learning.

26. Yo-Yo Ma: World-renowned cellist Yo-Yo Ma has emphasized the importance of arts education and its impact on creativity and cultural understanding.

27. Oprah Winfrey: Media mogul Oprah Winfrey has consistently promoted the value of education and its ability to empower individuals and communities.

28. Michelle Pfeiffer: Actress Michelle Pfeiffer has emphasized the importance of education and the opportunities it can create.

29. Larry Page: Co-founder of Google, Larry Page has emphasized the importance of education in fostering innovation and driving technological advancements.

30. Andrew Cuomo: Former Governor of New York Andrew Cuomo has advocated for affordable higher education and expanded access for students.

31. Misty Copeland: Ballet dancer Misty Copeland has spoken about the role of education in pursuing one's passions and achieving success.

32. Howard Schultz: Former CEO of Starbucks, Howard Schultz has emphasized the value of education in building a strong workforce and promoting social mobility.

33. Sonia Sotomayor: Supreme Court Justice Sonia Sotomayor has emphasized the role of education in providing opportunities and empowering individuals.

34. Larry Ellison: Co-founder of Oracle Corporation, Larry Ellison has emphasized the importance of education in driving innovation and economic growth.

35. Melinda Gates: Philanthropist and co-founder of the Bill & Melinda Gates Foundation, Melinda Gates has focused on improving access to quality education globally.

36. James Cameron: Filmmaker James Cameron has spoken about the importance of education and its role in fostering creativity and critical thinking.

37. Arianna Huffington: Media entrepreneur Arianna Huffington has highlighted the importance of education in personal growth and well-being.

38. Malala Yousafzai: Nobel Peace Prize laureate Malala Yousafzai has continuously advocated for girls' education and the transformative power of education.

39. Richard Branson: Business magnate Richard Branson has emphasized the value of education in fostering entrepreneurship and innovation.

40. Colin Powell: Former U.S. Secretary of State Colin Powell has spoken about the importance of education in promoting global peace and understanding.

41. Maya Angelou: Poet and civil rights activist Maya Angelou believed in the power of education to break cycles of poverty and empower individuals.

42. Mark Zuckerberg: Co-founder and CEO of Facebook, Mark Zuckerberg has supported educational initiatives, including the Chan Zuckerberg Initiative focused on improving access to education.

These individuals represent just a few examples of famous figures who have voiced support for higher education and its transformative potential. Their advocacy reinforces the idea that higher education is a catalyst for personal growth, intellectual development, and societal progress, and that it plays a vital role in empowering individuals to create positive change in the world.

Things Employers SHOULD Do

While there may be instances where hiring someone without higher education training and background is appropriate, these points highlight the potential benefits of considering candidates who have completed higher education programs. Ultimately, hiring decisions should be based on a careful assessment of the specific requirements of the job, the skills and competencies of the candidates, and a consideration of the individual's overall potential for success in the role.

The process of hiring new employees is a critical decision for any organization. Employers strive to find candidates who possess the necessary skills, knowledge, and qualifications to excel in their roles. While some may argue that higher education is not a prerequisite for success, there are tangible costs associated with hiring individuals without higher education training and background. Together, we will explore the unnecessary costs that can arise from such hiring decisions and discuss the potential drawbacks for both employers and employees.

1. Limited Skillset and Competencies: One of the primary costs of hiring someone without higher education training is the limited skillset and competencies they may bring to

the table. Higher education equips individuals with specialized knowledge, practical skills, and critical thinking abilities that are essential for tackling complex challenges in the modern workplace. Without this foundation, employees may struggle to perform certain tasks, resulting in decreased productivity and potential errors that can have costly consequences for the organization.

2. Increased Training and Onboarding Needs: When hiring individuals without higher education training and background, employers often face the challenge of increased training and onboarding requirements. These employees may require additional time and resources to acquire the necessary skills and knowledge to perform their duties effectively. Consequently, organizations may need to allocate additional budget for training programs, mentorship, and professional development initiatives, which can strain financial resources and divert attention from other important business priorities.

3. Higher Turnover and Employee Dissatisfaction: Employees who lack higher education training and background may experience difficulties in adapting to their roles and meeting performance expectations. This can lead to higher turnover rates as individuals may feel unsatisfied or overwhelmed by their responsibilities. The cost of employee turnover is substantial, including recruitment expenses, lost productivity during the transition period, and the need to invest in training and integrating new hires into the organization. Employers may find themselves caught in a cycle of constant hiring and onboarding, resulting in unnecessary financial strain.

4. Limited Advancement Opportunities: Without a higher education background, individuals may face limitations in their career growth and advancement opportunities within the organization. Many roles require specific qualifications and educational achievements for promotions or senior-level positions. Hiring individuals without higher education training may result in a workforce lacking the necessary qualifications to take on higher-level responsibilities. This can lead to a lack of

internal talent development and the need to recruit externally, incurring additional recruitment and onboarding costs.

5. Reduced Innovation and Problem-Solving Capabilities: Higher education fosters critical thinking, research skills, and innovation, which are vital for organizations to stay competitive in a rapidly evolving marketplace. Hiring individuals without higher education training may result in a lack of diverse perspectives, fresh ideas, and innovative approaches to problem-solving. This can hinder organizational growth, limit creativity, and impede the ability to adapt to changing market dynamics, ultimately costing the organization opportunities for growth and innovation.

6. Decreased Competitive Advantage: In today's competitive job market, organizations strive to gain a competitive edge by attracting top talent. Many highly skilled and motivated candidates pursue higher education to enhance their qualifications and marketability. By overlooking candidates with higher education training, organizations may lose out on individuals who possess a deeper understanding of industry trends,

advanced skills, and a demonstrated commitment to continuous learning. This can diminish the organization's ability to stay ahead of competitors and hamper long-term success.

7. Impact on Company Reputation: Hiring decisions can influence an organization's reputation and perception among potential employees, clients, and stakeholders. A company that consistently overlooks the value of higher education may be viewed as lacking in progressive thinking, professionalism, and commitment to excellence. Such perceptions can affect recruitment efforts, client relationships, and overall brand reputation, potentially leading to financial setbacks and missed opportunities for growth.

8. Diminished Employee Morale: When highly qualified employees with higher education training observe colleagues without similar qualifications being hired for similar roles, it can lead to decreased morale and dissatisfaction. This disparity can create an environment of perceived inequality, as qualified employees may question the organization's commitment to recognizing

their efforts and investments in higher education. Such negative sentiments can negatively impact team dynamics, collaboration, and overall employee engagement, ultimately affecting productivity and organizational performance.

9. Limited Access to Professional Networks: Higher education institutions often provide students with access to a vast network of alumni, professors, and industry professionals. This network can be invaluable for career opportunities, mentorship, and professional growth. By overlooking candidates with higher education backgrounds, organizations may miss out on the potential benefits of tapping into these established networks, limiting their ability to connect with influential individuals and gain access to valuable resources.

10. Compliance with Industry Standards and Regulations: Certain industries have specific requirements and regulations that necessitate employees with higher education training and credentials. Hiring individuals without the necessary qualifications can result in non-compliance with legal and industry standards, potentially leading to penalties,

legal disputes, and reputational damage. Employers must consider the potential legal and financial risks associated with hiring individuals who lack the required educational background for certain positions.

While there may be exceptions where hiring individuals without higher education training and background is justified, organizations should carefully consider the associated costs and potential drawbacks. The limitations in skills, increased training needs, higher turnover rates, diminished innovation, reduced competitive advantage, impact on company reputation, and employee morale are factors that can lead to unnecessary financial strain and hinder long-term success.

1. **Depth of Knowledge:** Higher education provides individuals with in-depth knowledge and expertise in their chosen field. This depth of knowledge allows them to approach complex problems and challenges with a comprehensive understanding, enabling more effective decision-making and problem-solving.

2. **Specialized Skills:** Higher education programs often offer specialized training,

equipping individuals with specific skills that are valuable in their respective fields. These skills can be difficult to acquire outside of an educational setting and can give candidates a competitive edge.

3. **Critical Thinking Abilities:** Higher education fosters critical thinking skills, enabling individuals to analyze information, evaluate different perspectives, and make informed judgments. This ability is crucial for complex problem-solving, innovation, and decision-making.

4. **Research and Analytical Skills:** Higher education emphasizes research and analytical skills, enabling individuals to gather, evaluate, and interpret data effectively. These skills are essential in fields that require evidence-based decision-making, such as scientific research, policy analysis, and market research.

5. **Adaptability and Lifelong Learning:** Higher education instills a mindset of adaptability and lifelong learning. Graduates are equipped with the ability to quickly acquire new knowledge, adapt to changing

circumstances, and stay updated with the latest industry trends and advancements.

6. **Professional Network:** Higher education institutions provide opportunities to build a professional network, connecting students with professors, alumni, and industry professionals. These connections can be valuable for mentorship, career guidance, and future employment opportunities.

7. **Demonstrated Commitment and Discipline:** Completing a higher education program demonstrates an individual's commitment, discipline, and ability to work towards long-term goals. This dedication is often valued by employers as it indicates a strong work ethic and the ability to follow through on commitments.

8. **Strong Work Ethic:** Higher education requires students to manage multiple assignments, meet deadlines, and juggle various responsibilities. This experience helps develop a strong work ethic that can positively impact job performance and productivity.

9. **Breadth of Knowledge:** Higher education provides a well-rounded education, exposing students to a wide range of subjects and disciplines. This breadth of knowledge can help individuals make connections across different fields, think creatively, and approach problems from multiple perspectives.

10. **Effective Communication Skills:** Higher education often emphasizes effective written and oral communication skills. Graduates are better equipped to articulate their ideas, collaborate with colleagues, and convey complex information to diverse audiences.

11. **Ethical Considerations:** Higher education promotes an understanding of ethical principles and fosters a sense of social responsibility. This awareness can influence decision-making, professionalism, and integrity in the workplace.

12. **Professional Credentials:** In certain professions, a higher education degree is a prerequisite for obtaining professional credentials and licenses. Hiring individuals with the necessary credentials can ensure

compliance with legal and regulatory requirements.

13. **Problem-Solving Abilities:** Higher education equips individuals with the ability to identify problems, analyze root causes, and develop effective solutions. This skill set is invaluable in roles that involve innovation, process improvement, and strategic planning.

14. **Leadership Potential:** Higher education often provides opportunities for leadership development through extracurricular activities, group projects, and student organizations. This experience can help identify individuals with strong leadership potential and the ability to inspire and motivate others.

15. **Global Perspective:** Higher education encourages exposure to diverse cultures, perspectives, and global issues. Graduates are more likely to possess a global mindset, cross-cultural understanding, and the ability to work effectively in diverse teams.

Things Employers Should NOT Do

These are some reasons why hiring someone without higher education training and background may not be advantageous in certain contexts. It is important to note that these reasons may vary depending on the specific industry, job requirements, and individual circumstances. Here are some key points to consider:

1. Lack of specialized knowledge: Higher education provides individuals with specialized knowledge and expertise in their chosen fields, which may be essential for certain roles.

2. Limited critical thinking abilities: Higher education fosters critical thinking skills, enabling individuals to analyze information, evaluate different perspectives, and make informed decisions.

3. Inadequate research and analytical skills: Higher education emphasizes research and analytical skills, which are crucial for evidence-based decision-making and problem-solving.

4. Limited exposure to industry practices: Higher education programs often incorporate real-world experiences and internships, giving students exposure to industry practices that may be lacking in those without such training.

5. Inability to adapt to complex challenges: Higher education equips individuals with the ability to adapt to complex challenges by providing them with a breadth of knowledge and the skills necessary to navigate various situations.

6. Lack of a strong professional network: Higher education institutions provide opportunities for students to build a professional network, which can be valuable for mentorship, career guidance, and future employment opportunities.

7. Less demonstrated commitment and discipline: Completing a higher education program demonstrates an individual's commitment, discipline, and ability to work towards long-term goals.

8. Limited breadth of knowledge: Higher education provides individuals with a well-rounded education, exposing them to a wide range of subjects and disciplines that may enhance their understanding and problem-solving abilities.

9. Insufficient communication skills: Higher education often emphasizes effective written and oral communication skills, which are vital for collaboration and conveying complex information.

10. Lack of exposure to diverse perspectives: Higher education encourages exposure to diverse cultures, perspectives, and global issues, fostering cross-cultural understanding and the ability to work effectively in diverse teams.

11. Limited leadership potential: Higher education offers opportunities for leadership development, enabling individuals to acquire the skills necessary to inspire and motivate others.

12. Less adaptability and lifelong learning mindset: Higher education instills a mindset of adaptability and lifelong learning, which is

essential for staying updated with industry trends and advancements.

13. Inadequate understanding of ethical considerations: Higher education promotes an understanding of ethical principles and fosters a sense of social responsibility, which can influence decision-making and professionalism in the workplace.

14. Lack of professional credentials: In some professions, a higher education degree is a requirement for obtaining professional credentials and licenses.

15. Limited problem-solving abilities: Higher education equips individuals with problem-solving skills, enabling them to identify and analyze problems and develop effective solutions.

16. Inability to handle complex information: Higher education provides individuals with the ability to handle complex information and synthesize it into meaningful insights.

17. Lack of familiarity with industry standards: Higher education programs often expose students to industry standards, practices, and

emerging trends, giving them a competitive edge in the job market.

18. Limited understanding of global perspectives: Higher education encourages exposure to global issues, fostering a global mindset and an understanding of diverse cultures.

19. Inadequate exposure to interdisciplinary approaches: Higher education encourages interdisciplinary learning, enabling individuals to draw from multiple disciplines to address complex challenges.

20. Less awareness of industry-specific tools and technologies: Higher education programs often provide hands-on experience with industry-specific tools and technologies, which may be crucial for certain job roles.

It's important to note that these reasons may not be applicable in all circumstances, and hiring decisions should be made on a case-by-case basis, considering the specific requirements of the role, the skills and competencies of the candidates, and the individual's potential for success.

100 Similar Words - Higher Education

- Advanced education
- Tertiary education
- Postsecondary education
- University
- College
- Academia
- Institution of higher learning
- Higher learning
- Further education
- Vocational education
- Professional education
- Graduate school
- Liberal arts education
- Technical training
- Career development
- Intellectual development
- Academic pursuit
- Learning beyond high school
- Scholarly pursuit
- Knowledge advancement
- Intellectual growth
- Educational attainment
- Academic excellence
- Intellectual exploration
- Lifelong learning
- Career preparation

- Skill development
- Personal growth
- Intellectual development
- Specialized education
- Continuing education
- Advanced studies
- Research-based education
- Academic achievement
- Specialized training
- Vocational training
- Professional development
- Applied learning
- Practical education
- Technical education
- Research university
- Higher level of education
- Academic progression
- Intellectual enrichment
- Learning opportunities
- Academic culture
- Degree-granting institution
- Scholarly community
- Educational institution
- Intellectual pursuits
- Pedagogical engagement
- Academic environment
- Intellectual pursuits
- Educational enrichment
- Academic rigor

- Scholarly endeavors
- Knowledge acquisition
- Intellectual inquiry
- Academic sphere
- Educational sector
- Academic world
- Learning institutions
- Higher-level studies
- Intellectual endeavors
- Academic scholarship
- Higher education system
- Educational establishment
- Academic society
- Knowledge dissemination
- Intellectual accomplishments
- Educational progression
- Academic discipline
- Advanced learning
- Research and education
- Academic pursuits
- Higher education sector
- Educational landscape
- Intellectual pursuits
- Academic research
- Educational development
- Scholarly activities
- Academic community
- Intellectual engagement
- Educational sphere

- Academic resources
- Scholarly initiatives
- Knowledge exploration
- Educational advancements
- Academic infrastructure
- Intellectual challenges
- Educational opportunities
- Academic exploration
- Scholarly endeavors
- Learning and growth
- Intellectual endeavors
- Educational enrichment
- Academic growth
- Scholarly achievements
- Knowledge expansions
- Intellectual Stimulation

List of 500 Careers by Profession and Industry

1. Accountant
2. Architect
3. Aerospace engineer
4. Anesthesiologist
5. Attorney
6. Biomedical scientist
7. Business analyst
8. Chef
9. Civil engineer
10. Computer programmer
11. Content creator (YouTuber, Blogger)
12. Data analyst
13. Dentist
14. Digital marketer
15. Electrical engineer
16. Entrepreneur
17. Event planner
18. Financial advisor
19. Graphic designer
20. Human resources manager
21. Investment banker
22. Journalist
23. Marketing manager
24. Nurse
25. Occupational therapist
26. Pharmacist

27. Physical therapist
28. Physician
29. Police officer
30. Product manager
31. Project manager
32. Psychologist
33. Real estate agent
34. Registered nurse
35. Sales representative
36. Software engineer
37. Surgeon
38. Teacher
39. Veterinarian
40. Web developer

Furthermore, here are more examples of jobs and careers in various sectors:

Finance and Banking: 41. Actuary

42. Bank manager
43. Credit analyst
44. Financial analyst
45. Hedge fund manager
46. Insurance underwriter
47. Investment analyst
48. Mortgage broker
49. Private equity associate
50. Stockbroker

Technology and IT: 51. Artificial Intelligence (AI) engineer

52. Cybersecurity analyst
53. Data scientist
54. Full-stack developer
55. Machine learning engineer
56. Network administrator
57. Quality assurance analyst
58. Software architect
59. Systems analyst
60. User experience (UX) designer

Healthcare and Medicine: 61. Cardiologist

62. Clinical psychologist
63. Genetic counselor
64. Medical researcher
65. Neurologist
66. Nurse practitioner
67. Oncologist
68. Pediatrician
69. Pharmacist
70. Physical therapist

Business and Management: 71. Chief executive officer (CEO)

72. Chief financial officer (CFO)
73. Chief operating officer (COO)
74. General manager
75. Human resources director
76. Management consultant
77. Operations manager
78. Retail store manager
79. Supply chain manager
80. Venture capitalist

Creative and Media: 81. Art director

82. Film director
83. Interior designer
84. Photographer
85. Public relations manager
86. Social media manager
87. Video game designer
88. Visual effects artist
89. Writer or author

Engineering and Construction: 90. Chemical engineer

91. Civil engineer
92. Environmental engineer

93. Mechanical engineer
94. Petroleum engineer
95. Structural engineer
96. Surveyor
97. Urban planner
98. Water resource engineer
99. Wind turbine technician
100. Zoologist

Science and Research: 101. Astrophysicist

102. Biotechnologist
103. Chemist
104. Ecologist
105. Epidemiologist
106. Forensic scientist
107. Marine biologist
108. Materials scientist
109. Microbiologist
110. Research scientist

Education and Academia: 111. College professor

112. Dean of students
113. Education administrator
114. Elementary school teacher
115. High school principal
116. Librarian
117. School counselor

118. Special education teacher
119. Student affairs coordinator
120. University registrar

Government and Public Service: 121. Diplomat

122. Government policy analyst
123. Intelligence analyst
124. Nonprofit manager
125. Political campaign manager
126. Public health administrator
127. Social worker
128. Urban planner
129. U.S. Foreign Service officer
130. Zoning inspector

Hospitality and Tourism: 131. Concierge

132. Event manager
133. Hotel manager
134. Restaurant owner
135. Sommelier
136. Tour guide
137. Travel agent
138. Wedding planner
139. Winemaker
140. Yacht charter broker

Media and Entertainment: 141. Actor/Actress

    142.   Casting director
    143.   Film producer
    144.   Music producer
    145.   Radio host
    146.   Screenwriter
    147.   Sound engineer
    148.   Television producer
    149.   Voice-over artist
    150.   Web series creator

Social Services and Nonprofit: 151. Child welfare advocate

    152.   Community organizer
    153.   Fundraising manager
    154.   Grant writer
    155.   Human rights advocate
    156.   Nonprofit program director
    157.   Policy analyst
    158.   Substance abuse counselor
    159.   Volunteer coordinator
    160.   Youth mentor

Retail and Sales: 161. Brand manager

    162.   E-commerce specialist
    163.   Fashion buyer

164. Market research analyst
165. Retail store owner
166. Sales manager
167. Visual merchandiser
168. Wholesale distributor
169. Wine sales representative
170. Zone manager

Sports and Athletics: 171. Athletic coach

172. Fitness instructor
173. Professional athlete
174. Referee/Official
175. Sports agent
176. Sports psychologist
177. Sports broadcaster
178. Sports photographer
179. Sports therapist
180. Sports marketing manager

Environmental and Sustainability: 181. Climate change analyst

182. Conservation scientist
183. Environmental consultant
184. Green building architect
185. Renewable energy engineer
186. Sustainability manager
187. Waste management specialist

188. Water resource manager
189. Wildlife conservationist
190. Zero waste coordinator

Technology and Digital: 191. Artificial Intelligence (AI) specialist

192. Cloud architect
193. Cryptocurrency analyst
194. Data engineer
195. Ethical hacker
196. IT project manager
197. Mobile app developer
198. Robotics engineer
199. Software quality assurance (QA) engineer
200. User interface (UI) designer

Law and Legal Services: 201. Criminal defense attorney

202. Environmental lawyer
203. Immigration lawyer
204. Intellectual property lawyer
205. Judge
206. Legal consultant
207. Paralegal
208. Patent agent
209. Tax attorney

210. Trial lawyer

Finance and Investment: 211. Commodities trader

212. Financial planner
213. Hedge fund analyst
214. Investment banking associate
215. Personal financial advisor
216. Private banker
217. Risk analyst
218. Stock analyst
219. Venture capital associate
220. Wealth manager

Architecture and Design: 221. Landscape architect

222. Interior decorator
223. Sustainable design consultant
224. Urban designer
225. Lighting designer
226. Architectural historian
227. Exhibition designer
228. Furniture designer
229. Industrial designer
230. Set designer

Engineering and Manufacturing: 231. Aerospace engineer

- 232. Biomedical engineer
- 233. Chemical process engineer
- 234. Industrial engineer
- 235. Manufacturing engineer
- 236. Mining engineer
- 237. Power systems engineer
- 238. Quality control inspector
- 239. Robotics technician
- 240. Transportation engineer

Writing and Communication: 241. Copywriter

- 242. Editor
- 243. Grant writer
- 244. Journalist
- 245. Public relations specialist
- 246. Social media strategist
- 247. Technical writer
- 248. Translator
- 249. Video editor
- 250. Web content manager

Health and Wellness: 251. Acupuncturist

- 252. Chiropractor
- 253. Health coach

254. Holistic nutritionist
255. Massage therapist
256. Mental health counselor
257. Naturopathic doctor
258. Occupational therapist
259. Personal trainer
260. Yoga instructor

Aviation and Aerospace: 261. Air traffic controller

262. Aircraft maintenance technician
263. Aviation safety inspector
264. Flight attendant
265. Helicopter pilot
266. Aerospace engineer
267. Aircraft dispatcher
268. Aircraft sales representative
269. Aviation meteorologist
270. Drone operator

Marketing and Advertising: 271. Brand strategist

272. Content marketer
273. Digital advertising specialist
274. Market researcher
275. Media planner
276. Public relations manager
277. Search engine optimization (SEO) specialist

278. Social media manager
279. Web analytics manager
280. Influencer marketing manager

Nontraditional and Emerging Careers: 281. Artificial intelligence ethicist

282. Drone operator
283. Virtual reality (VR) developer
284. Cannabis industry professional
285. eSports athlete
286. Sustainability consultant
287. Data privacy consultant
288. Genealogist
289. Personal stylist
290. Voice actor

Education and Training: 291. Adult education instructor

292. Curriculum developer
293. Education consultant
294. Instructional designer
295. Learning and development specialist
296. School administrator
297. Student advisor
298. Test prep tutor
299. Vocational trainer
300. Workshop facilitator

Consulting: 301. Business consultant

302. Diversity and inclusion consultant
303. Environmental consultant
304. HR consultant
305. Management consultant
306. Marketing consultant
307. Organizational development consultant
308. Process improvement consultant
309. Strategy consultant
310. Sustainability consultant

Research and Analysis: 311. Data analyst

312. Economic analyst
313. Market researcher
314. Operations research analyst
315. Policy analyst
316. Quantitative analyst
317. Social researcher
318. Statistical analyst
319. Trend analyst
320. UX research analyst

Human Resources: 321. Compensation and benefits manager

322. Employee relations specialist

323. HR business partner
324. HR generalist
325. HR manager
326. Recruitment specialist
327. Talent acquisition manager
328. Training and development manager
329. Workforce planning analyst
330. HRIS analyst

Sports and Recreation: 331. Athletic director

332. Fitness center manager
333. Golf instructor
334. Personal trainer
335. Professional coach
336. Sports agent
337. Sports marketing manager
338. Sports therapist
339. Sports journalist
340. Sports event coordinator

Energy and Sustainability: 341. Energy engineer

342. Environmental engineer
343. Green building consultant
344. Renewable energy specialist
345. Sustainability coordinator
346. Environmental compliance officer
347. Energy auditor

348. Waste management consultant
349. Carbon footprint analyst
350. Sustainable transportation planner

Social Media and Influencer: 351. Social media manager

352. Content creator/influencer
353. Digital marketing specialist
354. Social media strategist
355. Brand ambassador
356. Community manager
357. Influencer agent
358. Social media analyst
359. Content curator
360. Social media advertising manager

Logistics and Supply Chain: 361. Logistics coordinator

362. Operations manager
363. Supply chain analyst
364. Warehouse manager
365. Distribution manager
366. Freight broker
367. Inventory control specialist
368. Procurement manager
369. Transportation planner
370. Supply chain consultant

Fashion and Retail: 371. Fashion designer

372.	Fashion merchandiser
373.	Retail buyer
374.	Visual merchandiser
375.	Fashion stylist
376.	Fashion photographer
377.	Store manager
378.	E-commerce manager
379.	Fashion PR specialist
380.	Retail sales associate

Music and Performing Arts: 381. Composer

382.	Music producer
383.	Orchestra conductor
384.	Music therapist
385.	Music teacher
386.	Sound engineer
387.	Stage director
388.	Choreographer
389.	Casting director
390.	Music event manager

Culinary Arts and Hospitality: 391. Executive chef

392.	Pastry chef
393.	Sommelier
394.	Restaurant manager

395. Catering manager
396. Food and beverage director
397. Hotel operations manager
398. Resort manager
399. Food critic
400. Culinary instructor

Law Enforcement and Security: 401. Border patrol agent

402. Correctional officer
403. Criminal investigator
404. Customs and immigration officer
405. FBI agent
406. Intelligence analyst
407. Private detective
408. Secret Service agent
409. Security manager
410. Police detective

Architecture and Urban Planning: 411. City planner

412. Landscape designer
413. Architectural historian
414. Urban designer
415. Urban planner
416. Building surveyor
417. Historic preservation specialist
418. Sustainable design architect

419. Interior architect
420. Urban regeneration consultant

Public Health and Healthcare Administration: 421. Epidemiologist

422. Health services manager
423. Healthcare consultant
424. Health informatics specialist
425. Medical administrator
426. Public health educator
427. Health policy analyst
428. Healthcare compliance officer
429. Health program coordinator
430. Healthcare data analyst

Publishing and Writing: 431. Editor

432. Literary agent
433. Copy editor
434. Freelance writer
435. Book publisher
436. Literary critic
437. Proofreader
438. Technical writer
439. Content strategist
440. Publishing manager

Social Sciences and Humanities: 441. Anthropologist

442. Economist
443. Historian
444. Political scientist
445. Psychologist
446. Sociologist
447. Archaeologist
448. Linguist
449. Ethnographer
450. Philosopher

Entrepreneurship and Startups: 451. Startup founder

452. Business development manager
453. Venture capitalist
454. Product manager
455. Social entrepreneur
456. Innovation consultant
457. Angel investor
458. Growth hacker
459. Franchise owner
460. Business coach

Film and Television Production: 461. Film director

462. Cinematographer

463. Film editor
464. Production designer
465. Sound designer
466. Costume designer
467. Casting director
468. Film producer
469. Script supervisor
470. Location manager

Environmental Conservation and Advocacy: 471. Conservation biologist

472. Environmental policy analyst
473. Ecotourism manager
474. Sustainability officer
475. Wildlife biologist
476. Environmental educator
477. Forest ranger
478. Climate change researcher
479. Environmental lawyer
480. Greenpeace campaigner

International Relations and Diplomacy: 481. Diplomat

482. Foreign service officer
483. International development consultant
484. Global affairs analyst
485. Humanitarian aid worker

486. Conflict resolution specialist
487. International trade specialist
488. Political risk analyst
489. International lawyer
490. Diplomatic interpreter

Research and Development: 491. Research scientist

492. Laboratory technician
493. Data scientist
494. Research and development engineer
495. Research analyst
496. Clinical research coordinator
497. Product development manager
498. Quality assurance analyst
499. Usability researcher
500. R&D director

Thought Provoking Quote

By

Dr. Lester G. Reid

The statement, "If you have been to college and you have never had a transformational experience, then you haven't been to college, you only passed through," implies that a true college experience goes beyond merely attending classes and completing academic requirements. It suggests that the transformative power of higher education lies in the personal growth, self-discovery, and meaningful experiences that one gains during their time in college.

When someone "passes through" college without experiencing transformation, it means they may have focused solely on fulfilling academic obligations without fully engaging in the broader opportunities available to them. These opportunities include participating in extracurricular activities, joining clubs or organizations, engaging in research or internships, building relationships with peers and faculty members, and exploring new perspectives and ideas.

A transformational college experience involves more than acquiring knowledge; it involves personal development, broadening one's horizons, and developing skills and qualities that extend beyond the academic realm. It is about embracing the diverse range of experiences and opportunities that college offers, challenging oneself intellectually, and growing as an individual.

Transformational experiences in college can take many forms. They may include participating in community service projects that foster empathy and social responsibility, studying abroad and gaining a global perspective, conducting research that deepens understanding and critical thinking skills, or engaging in discussions and debates that challenge one's beliefs and broaden one's worldview.

These experiences can lead to personal growth, increased self-confidence, and the development of important life skills such as communication, critical thinking, problem-solving, and leadership. They also contribute to the formation of lifelong friendships and connections, and they can shape one's future career path and goals.

However, it is important to note that the transformative nature of college experiences can vary from person to person. Not everyone will have the same transformative journey, and it is not a measure of the value of their college education. Some individuals may find transformation in small, subtle ways, while others may have profound and life-altering experiences. The key is to be open to new opportunities, actively seek personal growth, and engage in the various aspects of college life beyond academics.

The statement emphasizes that a truly transformative college experience goes beyond fulfilling academic requirements. It involves actively engaging in personal growth, self-discovery, and meaningful experiences that expand one's knowledge, skills, and perspectives. By embracing all that college has to offer, individuals can truly benefit from the transformative power of higher education.

References

1. Astin, A. W. (1993). What Matters in College?: Four Critical Years Revisited. Jossey-Bass.
2. Carnevale, A. P., Smith, N., & Strohl, J. (2013). Recovery: Job Growth and Education Requirements through 2020. Georgetown University Center on Education and the Workforce.
3. Autor, D. H. (2014). Skills, education, and the rise of earnings inequality among the "other 99 percent". Science, 344(6186), 843-851.
4. Chetty, R., Friedman, J. N., Saez, E., Turner, N., & Yagan, D. (2017). Mobility report cards: The role of colleges in intergenerational mobility. National Bureau of Economic Research.
5. Heckman, J. J., Humphries, J. E., & Veramendi, G. (2020). Returns to education: The causal effects of education on earnings, health, and smoking. Journal of Political Economy, 128(3), 729-798.
6. Perna, L. W., & Titus, M. A. (2005). The relationship between parental involvement as social capital and college enrollment: An examination of racial/ethnic group

differences. The Journal of Higher Education, 76(5), 485-518.
7. Krueger, A. B. (1999). Experimental estimates of education production functions. The Quarterly Journal of Economics, 114(2), 497-532.
8. Beegle, K., Dehejia, R., & Gatti, R. (2009). Why should we care about child labor? The education, labor market, and health consequences of child labor. Journal of Human Resources, 44(4), 871-889.
9. Goldin, C., & Katz, L. F. (2008). The race between education and technology. Harvard University Press.
10. Heckman, J. J., Stixrud, J., & Urzua, S. (2006). The effects of cognitive and noncognitive abilities on labor market outcomes and social behavior. Journal of Labor Economics, 24(3), 411-482.
11. Baum, S., & Ma, J. (2018). Trends in College Pricing 2018. The College Board.
12. Hout, M. (2012). Social and economic returns to college education in the United States. Annual Review of Sociology, 38, 379-400.
13. Oreopoulos, P., & Petronijevic, U. (2013). Making college worth it: A review of research on the returns to higher education. The Future of Children, 23(1), 41-65.

14. Card, D. (1999). The causal effect of education on earnings. Handbook of Labor Economics, 3, 1801-1863.
15. Acemoglu, D., & Autor, D. H. (2011). Skills, tasks and technologies: Implications for employment and earnings. Handbook of Labor Economics, 4, 1043-1171.
16. Hoxby, C. M. (2018). The returns to online postsecondary education. Brookings Papers on Economic Activity, Spring 2018, 309-366.
17. Dynarski, S., & Scott-Clayton, J. (2013). Financial aid policy: Lessons from research. The Future of Children, 23(1), 67-91.
18. Bureau of Labor Statistics. (2021). Occupational Outlook Handbook. U.S. Department of Labor.
19. Smeeding, T. M., & Thompson, J. P. (Eds.). (2011). Persistence, privilege, and parenting: The comparative study of intergenerational mobility. Russell Sage Foundation.
20. Hershbein, B., & Kearney, M. S. (2014). Major decisions: What graduates earn over their lifetimes. NBER Working Paper No. 19331.
21. Autor, D. H. (2010). The polarization of job opportunities in the US labor market: Implications for employment and earnings.

Center for American Progress and The Hamilton Project.
22. Bureau of Labor Statistics. (2021). Education pays: Earnings and unemployment rates by educational attainment. U.S. Department of Labor.
23. Chetty, R., Friedman, J. N., & Rockoff, J. E. (2014). Measuring the impacts of teachers II: Teacher value-added and student outcomes in adulthood. The Quarterly Journal of Economics, 129(3), 1321-1376.
24. Carnevale, A. P., Smith, N., & Gulish, A. (2019). The economic value of college majors. Georgetown University Center on Education and the Workforce.
25. Autor, D. H. (2014). Skills, education, and the rise of earnings inequality among the "other 99 percent". Science, 344(6186), 843-851.
26. Mason, M. A., & Ekman, R. (2019). The Future of Graduate Education: Challenges and Opportunities. American Academy of Arts & Sciences.
27. Carnevale, A. P., & Strohl, J. (2010). Help wanted: Projections of jobs and education requirements through 2018. Georgetown University Center on Education and the Workforce.

28. Chetty, R., Friedman, J. N., & Rockoff, J. E. (2014). Measuring the impacts of teachers II: Teacher value-added and student outcomes in adulthood. The Quarterly Journal of Economics, 129(3), 1321-1376.
29. Krueger, A. B., & Dale, S. B. (2002). Estimating the payoff to attending a more selective college: An application of selection on observables and unobservables. The Quarterly Journal of Economics, 117(4), 1491-1527.
30. Carnoy, M., & Rhoten, D. (Eds.). (2002). The global transformation of higher education. Stanford University Press.

ABOUT THE AUTHOR

Dr. Lester Reid is a distinguished expert in the fields of higher education, human development, training and development, business development, career coaching, executive coaching, accounting and finance, federal taxation, research and publication, education, facilitation, transformational speaking, transformational leadership, and an inspirational figure. With a wealth of knowledge and experience in these areas, Dr. Reid has made a significant impact on individuals, organizations, and communities through his expertise, guidance, and transformative approach.

As a leader in the field of human development, Dr. Reid has devoted his career to empowering individuals to reach their full potential. He understands that personal growth and development are essential components of a fulfilling and successful life. Through his transformative approach, he helps individuals identify their strengths, overcome obstacles, and unlock their innate talents and abilities. Dr. Reid's expertise in training and development enables him to design and deliver impactful programs that inspire personal and professional growth.

Dr. Lester Reid is an inspirational figure who has dedicated his life to higher education, human development, training and development, business development, career coaching, executive coaching, accounting and finance, federal taxation, research and publication, education, facilitation, transformational speaking, transformational leadership, and making a positive impact on the lives of others. Through his expertise, guidance, and transformative approach, he has helped individuals unlock their full potential, organizations achieve success, and communities thrive. Dr. Reid's contributions to these fields are invaluable, and his passion for empowering others serves as a beacon of inspiration to all who have the privilege of encountering his work.

www.ingramcontent.com/pod-product-compliance
Lightning Source LLC
LaVergne TN
LVHW051049080426
835508LV00019B/1788